# FROM

# SILENCE

# TO

# SONG

# FROM SILENCE TO SONG

The Davidic Liturgical Revolution

Peter J. Leithart

Canon Press ▦ *Moscow*

Peter J. Leithart, *From Silence to Song: The Davidic Liturgical Revolution*

© 2003 by Peter Leithart
Published by Canon Press, P.O. Box 8741, Moscow, ID 83843
800-488-2034 / www.canonpress.org
Printed in the United States of America.

Cover design by Paige Atwood.

03 04 05 06 07 08     9 8 7 6 5 4 3 2 1

*Library of Congress Cataloging-in-Publication Data*

Leithart, Peter J.
 From silence to song : the Davidic liturgical revolution / by Peter Leithart.
  p. cm.
Includes index.
 ISBN 1-59128-001-X (pbk.)
 1. Public worship in the Bible. 2. Bible. O.T. Samuel, 2nd, VI—Criticism, interpretation, etc. 3. Bible. O.T. Chronicles, 1st, XIII-XVI—Criticism, interpretation, etc. 4. David, King of Israel. 5. Tablernacle. 6. Public worship—Biblical teaching. 7. Reformed Church—Liturgy. I. Title.
 BS1325.6.P93 .L45 2002
 264—dc21
                                                    2002006519

# Contents

Preface ................................................................ 7

1. The Problem of Davidic Worship ..................... 11

2. According to the Pattern ............................... 19

3. Some for Priests and Levites ........................... 31

4. Sacrifices of Praise ....................................... 53

5. The Booth of David ...................................... 73

6. The Ends of Song ....................................... 101

Scripture Index ............................................. 131

# Preface

I have taught on the tabernacle of David in several venues during the past few years, and each time I have returned to it, it has grown bigger in my absence. The last time, I prefaced my lectures by saying that I was reporting on a work in progress. I have always felt that a great deal was still eluding me. Every now and then I have had the sense that, after huffing and puffing through the texts yet again, I was finally about to reach the peak, where I expected to gaze out vertiginously at a vast new undiscovered territory spreading out before me to the horizon—a fruitful land and green.

Alas. It is still getting bigger, and I still feel that the peak is a ways ahead, somewhere up there through the fog. And that means that this book is also a "report on a work in progress" rather than a definitive treatment of the subject. There are large holes in this book. Occasionally, I have set a fence around my open pits, dutifully attaching florescent orange warning signs. Other times, I have left it to the reader to discover the gaps in the argument. In other cases, I have left no warning signs because I do not even know where all the danger spots are. *Caveat lector*, lest he tumble in unawares, never to be heard from again.

Why is it such a big deal? Maybe it is not, as a skeptical (and cruel) friend once said.

Undaunted, I insist it is a big deal. It is big because the tabernacle
of David was Yahweh's first dwelling in Jerusalem, which came to
be called the city of the great King. It is big because David's tent was
the only sanctuary *ever* established on Mount Zion, and because
Zion is one of the main symbols in Scripture. It is big because David
is arguably the central character of the Old Testament and certainly,
with Adam, one of the two chief Old Testament types of Jesus, and
because according to Chronicles his greatest achievement was the
reorganization of worship in preparation for the temple. It is big
because it was the moment when song began to play a large and even
dominant role in worship. It is big because it is the climactic image in the prophecy of Amos, one of the earliest prophetic books.
It is big because James talked about it at the first church council,
quoting that prophecy from Amos. It is big because it foreshad-
owed the joyful heavenly assembly to which we ascend in worship,
which in turn is a foretaste of the assembly at the end of all things.

If I am right, then I have written a small book on a big subject.
I have offered a map of the territory before reaching the summit.
Perhaps this book will turn out to be nothing more than a cry for
help from a distressed climber, in which case I expect a rescue party
to be dispatched immediately. But I hope for better. I hope readers, including that skeptical friend, will get some sense of the scale
of the subject. And, if I have misrepresented the topography, I hope
at least that I have made my path of ascent plain enough (with foot-
prints, markers, and discarded candy wrappers) so that someone else
might follow, someone with the skill and stamina actually to reach
the top.

*       *       *

I first lectured on the tabernacle of David in 1998, at a conference
sponsored by Westminster Presbyterian Church, Vancouver, Wash-
ington, and am grateful to Rev. James Bordwine and the session of
Westminster for the opportunity to speak there. At the Ministerial
Conference sponsored by Christ Church in Moscow, Idaho, in the

fall of 2000, I gave three lectures on the tabernacle of David and its implications for church music, and was greatly helped by the comments and questions posed by the participants and greatly encouraged by many of the responses. Finally, I lectured on the tabernacle of David at the Eleventh Annual Biblical Horizons Summer Conference in July 2001, and the interaction there helped me to formulate more precisely what I had to say on the subject.

A number of individuals have also encouraged this work and helped my research and writing in various ways. I met Chris Hoops at the 1998 conference at Westminster, and, being a former charismatic, he was intrigued to hear a Reformed theologian talking about the tabernacle of David. Chris has been enthusiastic about the work ever since, sent a book for my perusal, and alerted me to a web site on the subject. In the evening following the Christ Church Ministerial Conference, I sat in my smoke-filled library as Pastor Dennis Turri and members of Reformation Covenant Church pelted me with challenging questions and comments. Dennis later helped my research by sending me material on the tabernacle of David from a book edited by Robert Webber. Pastor Galen Sorey heard my lectures at the Biblical Horizons conference and was kind enough to find me a battered copy of Graham Truscott's *The Power of His Presence*, one of the few book-length discussions of the tabernacle of David.

Thanks also to Nate Smith, who searched out and photocopied articles from libraries in the St. Louis area, and to Jim Jordan, whose comments proved illuminating as always. I am grateful to Doug Jones for his willingness to consider the book for Canon Press.

This book is dedicated to my fifth son and namesake, James. Though at nine, he will not appreciate this book for some time to come, and perhaps never, he will nonetheless be delighted to see his name in print and to learn that I was able to work "Og, King of Bashan" into the text (though, try as I might, I found no place for Tintin). Whether he is appreciative or not, I dedicate this book to him knowing that he is a member of that joyful assembly on Zion, and hopeful that we shall spend eternity together singing the Song of Moses and of the Lamb.

Peniel Hall
Trinity Season 2001

# 1
# The Problem of Davidic Worship

That day, the dusty road leading into Jerusalem and up into the stronghold of Zion[1] was packed. All the elders of Israel were there, and the children lining the road caught glimpses of David's mighty men, armor flashing in the sun, men whose exploits had been told at every hearth in the land. At the center of the procession was a cluster of Levites in their white linen robes, carrying the ark of the covenant, the throne of Yahweh, hidden from sight by layers of fabric. Every time they took six steps, they stopped to offer sacrifice before taking a seventh. The noise was deafening: the tumult of trumpets and horns, the splash of cymbals, the eerie aching melodies of harp and lyre, the drone of the Levitical singers. And at the head of the procession, David, the great King David, danced like a fool before his King, wearing a linen ephod.

When the procession reached Zion, the Levites took the ark into the tent that David had prepared for it, and then sacrifices

[1] The word *Zion* is used only in a handful of texts in the historical books of the Old Testament, and in every occurrence it refers to the stronghold, and not to the temple mount nor to the city as a whole (see 2 Sam. 5:7; 1 Kgs. 8:1; 1 Chr 11:5; 2 Chr. 5:2). Among recent commentators, P. Kyle McCarter (*II Samuel*, Anchor Bible [Garden City: Doubleday, 1984], 139) is the most explicit on this point: the Ophel hilltop on the eastern edge of the city "was 'the stronghold of Zion' or 'the City of David' in the strict sense . . . but as the city was extended, first north beyond the Ophel to include the temple mount (the present-day Haram esh-Sherif) and then west, the names 'Zion' and 'City of David' came to be used more broadly." Technically, the temple mount was not "Zion" but "Moriah" (2 Chr. 3:1), though a broader use is evident in the Psalms and prophets.

of peace offerings were slaughtered and every family was treated to a meal in the Lord's presence. They stood in wonder as David's new Levitical choir sang praises to Yahweh before the tent. After David blessed them, they returned home, hearts full of gladness.

No one could remember a procession or a celebration like this, and they had to reach back far into the memory of Israel for comparisons. It reminded some of stories they had read or heard about the procession following the exodus from Egypt, when Miriam took the timbrel and led the women in dance and song. Others thought of the procession that had encircled Jericho, the priests blowing trumpets before Yahweh's throne for six days until the Lord crumbled the city's walls. Yahweh, they concluded, was conquering another city, but this time in order to make it His own.

In an article on the "ark narrative" in Chronicles, Tamara Eskenazi concluded that the enthronement of Yahweh in Jerusalem was an event of "global, even cosmic significance." She goes on: "No other event in Chronicles, not even the dedication of the temple, is enshrined in such broad-reaching terms and imagery."[2] Few Israelites would have explained the event they witnessed as Eskenazi does, but as each family descended from the height of Zion in the light of the setting sun, many realized, however dimly, that something very big, something even bigger than they could grasp, had happened before their eyes.

And no wonder. By the time David became king, the throne of Yahweh had been in "exile" from Israel for a century. At the battle of Aphek, the Philistines captured the ark, and even though it was returned seven months later, it was sent to the home of Abinadab of Kiriath-jearim, a Gibeonite town in an area jointly settled by the tribes of Judah and Benjamin (1 Sam. 4:1–7:2).[3] After David conquered Jerusalem and made it his capital, he soon decided to bring the ark into the city to him. For the first time in a century, the ark

---

[2] "A Literary Approach to Chronicles' Ark Narrative in 1 Chronicles 13–16," in Astrid B. Beck, et. al., eds., *Fortunate the Eyes That See: Essays in Honor of David N. Freedman* (Grand Rapids: Eerdmans, 1995), 270.

[3] For details of the chronology, see my *Untitled: A Christian Commentary on the Book of Samuel* (Moscow: Canon, forthcoming).

was back where it belonged, in the midst of Israel, and for the first time ever it resided in Jerusalem. The "tent which David had pitched for it" (2 Sam. 6:17; 1 Chr. 16:1) was the first sanctuary that Israel ever established in Jerusalem, and it was the only place of worship ever set up on Zion.

Throughout David's reign, the ark remained in this tent, and David organized the Levites to worship there. Meanwhile, the Mosaic tabernacle (without the ark) continued to operate in Gibeon, some seven miles northwest of the capital (1 Chr. 16:39–43). Eventually, the ark was reunited with the rest of the tabernacle furniture in the temple of Solomon (1 Kgs. 8:1–11; 2 Chr. 5:2–14).

Christians have devoted much effort to understanding the typological and theological significance of the Mosaic tabernacle and the temple of Solomon, but comparatively little effort has been expended on study of the liturgical situation in the time of David or its implications for Christian worship.[4] The scholarly literature is relatively sparse. Commentators on Samuel and Chronicles of course mention David's tent and the worship performed there, but few articles and monographs have attempted to study it in detail.[5]

---

[4] I have found only two book-length treatments of the subject, both from charismatic writers: Graham Truscott, *The Power of His Presence: The Restoration of the Tabernacle of David* (Burbank, Calif.: World Map Press, 1969) and Kevin J. Conner, *The Tabernacle of David* (Portland, Ore.: Bible Temple-Conner Publications, 1976). Brief discussions may also be found in articles by Janice E. Leonard and Richard C. Leonard in Robert E. Webber, ed., *The Complete Library of Christian Worship* (Nashville, Tenn.: Star Song Publishing, 1993), vol. 1, and Philip Mauro, *The Hope of Israel* (Sterling, Va.: Grace Abounding Ministries, 1988), chap. 18. There are also several articles on the web site www.tabernacle-of-david.com. I wish to thank Pastor Dennis Turri for the material from Webber, and Chris Hoops for pointing me to this web site.

[5] There is a large body of work on the so-called "ark narrative" of 1–2 Samuel (consisting, it is claimed, of 1 Sam. 4–6 and 2 Samuel 6), but the book of Samuel says very little about the worship conducted at the tent of David. That material is found in 1 Chronicles, mainly in chapters 13–16, and on these chapters little scholarly literature is available. See, for confirmation, the paucity of items in the bibliographies provided in Roddy Braun's Word Biblical Commentary on these chapters (*1 Chronicles* [Waco: Word, 1986], 172, 180–181). Several more recent studies of the Chronicler's presentation of the reign of David are useful: Simon J. De Vries, "Moses and David as Cult Founders in Chronicles," *Journal of Biblical Literature* 107, no. 4 (1988): 619–639; John W. Wright, "The Founding Father: The Structure of the Chronicler's David Narrative," *Journal of Biblical Literature* 117, no. 1 (1998):

This book explores this moment in Israel's history, this moment
of divided worship, in an attempt to grasp the significance of
David's tent and its liturgy.[6]
Encouraged by suggestive comments like those of Eskenazi, I
have several reasons for suspecting that such an examination will
repay the time and effort. First, the ark-shrine of David, and the
worship that Israel performed there, marked a crucial advance in
Israel's liturgical history. From what we can learn in the Pentateuch,
Israel's worship in the Mosaic period was virtually silent. Verbal confession was required on the Day of Atonement (Lev. 16:21), and
we can infer that confession often accompanied the presentation of
animal offerings. Trumpets were blown over the morning and
evening ascension offerings (Num. 10:9–10), but no other liturgical music is explicitly mentioned. By contrast, as we shall see (chapter 4), the worship of the Davidic tabernacle was mainly worship
in song, and the Levitical choir and orchestra was later incorporated

45–59; and Eskenazi, "A Literary Approach to Chronicles' Ark Narrative in 1 Chronicles
13–16." Articles on specific topics in 1 Chronicles 13–16 have also appeared and will be
noted later. The most significant examination of this material is John W. Kleinig's *The Lord's
Song: The Basis, Function and Significance of Choral Music in Chronicles* (*JSOT* Supplement
#156; Sheffield: *JSOT* Press, 1993), on which I have heavily relied throughout this book.
Kleinig's excellent study does not, however, concentrate attention specifically on the Davidic
situation, but instead examines liturgical music both in David's time and at the temple. Thus,
it does not raise the specific redemptive-historical questions that I address in this volume,
especially in chapter 5. My thanks to James B. Jordan for informing me about Kleinig's book.
  [6] The failure to recognize the uniqueness of Davidic worship has led to some significant
confusions. It is often assumed, for example, that "Zion" is the name of the temple mount
pure and simple, but 2 Chronicles 3:1 makes clear that Solomon built the temple on Mount
Moriah, a distinct peak in Jerusalem. (I have discussed this issue at more length in an unpublished paper, "Where Was Ancient Zion?") Further, the significance of the temple imagery in many of the psalms has been misconstrued. It does not seem possible that Psalm
27, for instance, could be a psalm "of David," as the title indicates, since it mentions David's
desire to "dwell in the house of Yahweh all the days of my life" and to "meditate in his temple"
(v. 4). The temple was not built until Solomon's time, so it seems impossible that the attribution to David could be accurate. Most scholars simply dispense with the Davidic title,
claiming it represents a later editor's addition to the psalm. This conclusion makes little sense,
however, since the editor doubtless knew as well as we do that Solomon, not David, built the
temple; why would he sow confusion by attributing a temple psalm to David? We can go a
long way to solving this problem by recognizing that David began the process of temple construction by erecting the tent for the ark in Jerusalem. Though the temple was not yet built,
there was a sanctuary on Zion during David's time, and this was the foundation of the later
temple.

into temple worship in the days of Solomon. When Christians sing hymns and psalms in worship, when we play organs or pianos, guitars or trumpets, we are heirs of the Davidic "liturgical revolution."

Because David's reign saw the inception of worship through song, the portions of the Bible that describe this period, especially Chronicles, provide more material on worship music than any other section of the Bible. Attention to these passages will help to address both long-standing and contemporary debates about church music. Reformed liturgists have long debated the propriety of instrumental music in worship, for example, and there are no passages of Scripture more relevant to this question than those having to do with the Davidic tabernacle. Though I make no attempt to answer all of the specific questions that have been or are being debated throughout the church, I hope that this book provides some fresh directions for groping toward answers. If I provide few answers, I hope at least to provoke additional, and perhaps fundamental, questions.

Some liturgists, including Reformed liturgists, may object that I am looking in the wrong place for guidance concerning the theology and practice of Christian worship. Instead of examining the Old Testament, which describes a form of worship that has been fulfilled and set aside in Christ, we should concentrate on New Testament passages concerning worship, especially certain chapters of 1 Corinthians. Other liturgists seek guidance for Christian worship from the example of the Jewish synagogue, considered the origin and fount of Christian worship.[7] I address these objections at somewhat more length in the concluding chapter, but a word must be said at this point about the hermeneutical assumptions underlying the Reformed "regulative principle of worship." In the hands of at least some writers, the regulative principle is, in practice, hermeneutically wooden and theologically Marcionite.[8] It is wooden because

---

[7] I have addressed the question of synagogue worship as a model of Christian worship in "Synagogue or Temple? Models for Christian Worship," *Westminster Theological Journal* (forthcoming).

[8] Marcion was the early church heretic who believed that the god of the New Testament was a different deity from the god of the Old. I am using "Marcionite" in this context to describe

an explicit "command" is required for every act of worship, and it is Marcionite because it ignores the abundant Old Testament liturgical instruction in favor of exegeting a few passages of the New.

Refuting the Marcionite assumption must be left for another time, but the woodenness of "regulativism" is directly addressed by the passages studied in this book. As I will argue below, David's reorganization of worship at the tabernacle in Jerusalem was based on Mosaic ceremonial law, yet it was an expansive and creative application of the law, without ceasing to be an application. David's liturgical revolution thus provides a *canonical* illustration of how the law was applied in liturgical matters. By examining these portions of Scripture, furthermore, we can see that the church's "sacrifice of praise" grew out of an application of Levitical law. By showing the subtlety of the law's relation to Davidic worship, this study offers some hints about the scriptural regulation of worship in general and shows the relevance of Levitical liturgics to Christian worship (see chapter 6).

The Davidic system of worship is also important for understanding redemptive history, the hope of Israel as expressed by the prophets, and the fulfillment of this hope in the early church. Here the questions have to do with the redemptive logic of the history that we will be reviewing: Why did God set up His house in Jerusalem in this particular way? Why did He not move smoothly and directly from the Mosaic tabernacle to the Solomonic temple? Why tear the tabernacle apart first, and why separate the ark from the Mosaic tent for more than a century? Why set up an ark-shrine in Jerusalem for a generation before bringing the rest of the sanctuary to the capital city?

Amos 9:11–12, and specifically its use by James at the council of Jerusalem (Acts 15:16–18), makes it clear that the tabernacle of David was typologically significant. I argue in chapter 5 that Amos prophesied the restoration of the Davidic form of worship as well

---

a system of theology (in this case, liturgical theology) that sharply separates between the Old and New. See my discussion of the effect of Marcionite hermeneutics on sacramental theology in *The Priesthood of the Plebs: The Baptismal Transformation of Antique Order* (Eugene, Ore.: Wipf & Stock, forthcoming).

as the Davidic kingdom, and that James recognized that this restoration was taking place in the apostolic period. Its importance is
made even more evident when we recall that the Davidic tabernacle
was the only sanctuary ever established on Mount Zion. After
Solomon built the temple, he transferred the ark from Zion to
Moriah (2 Chr. 3:1), and in so doing transferred "Zion" and all its
associations to the temple. But the original significance of "Zion"
was not lost; the application of Zion language to the temple was an
extension of the Davidic system to the temple system. In short, the
Davidic tabernacle on Zion was somehow more fundamental to
Israel's worship, life, and future than the temple system.

Further, the prophets always use the language of Zion to describe
the future restoration of Jerusalem. Never once did an Old Testament prophet announce that "Moriah" would be raised up to be
chief of the mountains.[9] Always and everywhere, the promise is that
Zion will be exalted to become the praise of the earth. Along similar lines, the prophets never held out the hope for a restoration of
the glory of Solomon's reign; Solomon is mentioned only once in
the prophetic books, in Jeremiah 52, a narrative passage that is iden-
tical to the last chapter of 2 Kings. Instead, the prophetic hope always was framed in terms of a restored Davidic king, or of the
restoration of David himself to the throne of Israel.[10] Israel's
eschatology always focused on David, not Solomon, and Zion, not
Moriah. This striking emphasis will, I hope, make somewhat more
sense after we examine the features of and the worship at the ark-
sanctuary that was the center of Israel's worship during that time.

At many points in this book, I acknowledge that many of my
conclusions, both large and small, are tentative. But I hope at least
that I have given a plausible explanation for the excitement that attended that great procession into Zion on the day when David, the

---

[9] "Moriah" is used only in Genesis 22 and 2 Chronicles 3:1.

[10] It might be argued that Solomon's sins so tarnished his reign that the prophets could
not look to it as a model for the future, but David's sins were also grievous, and Israel achieved
its greatest international stature under Solomon, not David. It is also true that the prophetic
hope is often a hope for a "son of David," that is, a new Solomon; but that scion of David's
house is never called "Solomon," but always described in terms of David.

great King David, danced like a fool before the throne of his King, wearing a linen ephod.

# 2
# According to the Pattern

The establishment of Davidic worship is described in two passages of the Old Testament: 2 Samuel 6 and 1 Chronicles 13–16. I have dealt with the former passage in my commentary on Samuel[1] and will not repeat all of that material here. Several points should, however, be noted. First, Samuel as a whole represents David as the new Israel, and 2 Samuel 6 in particular is organized to highlight analogies between David's capture of Jerusalem and Joshua's conquest of Canaan. From this perspective, the establishment of the ark-shrine in Jerusalem was the endpoint of a renewed conquest (see Josh. 18:1). Related to the conquest theme, 2 Samuel 5–8 cycle through a "victory-housebuilding" sequence several times: First David or Yahweh fights and defeats an enemy, and then a house(hold) is built. From this angle, the ark-shrine represents the Divine Warrior's enthronement, His sabbatical rest after His triumph over Philistia. Within the larger context of the book of Samuel, this section continues the story that began in 1 Samuel 4–6 with the Philistine capture of the ark after the battle of Aphek. In 2 Samuel 6, the ark's "exile" is finally coming to a conclusion.

Chronicles, however, treats David's reign and the ascension of the ark to Zion in a very different manner. David is not presented

---

[1] *A Son to Me: An Exposition of I and II Samuel* (Moscow: Canon, forthcoming); see also my *A House for My Name: A Survey of the Old Testament* (Moscow: Canon, 2000), 140–149.

as a new Israel, and thus the establishment of the ark in Zion is not seen as the completion of a new conquest. The "victory-housebuilding" pattern appears in Chronicles, but is subordinated to other themes. And, since the Chronicler does not mention Aphek, the establishment of the ark in Jerusalem is not pictured as the reversal of Aphek. Not only does Chronicles set the story of the ark in a very different context from Samuel, but it also includes many details not found in the earlier book. Taking note of these differences will enable us to grasp the importance of David's tabernacle to the Chronicler.[2]

*Two Stories, One David*[3]

For starters, 1 Chronicles completely leaves out the conflicts between David and Saul and between David's house and Saul's house. While 1 Samuel devotes fifteen chapters to Saul's persecution of David (16–31), Chronicles recounts Saul's reign in one brief chapter (10:1–14), and the only event recorded is the battle of Gilboa at which Saul died. Further, 1 Chronicles leaves out the early years of David's reign when David was fighting with Saul's son Ish-

---

[2] Throughout this book, I use the contemporary convention of referring to the author of Chronicles as "the Chronicler." The traditional view that the author was Ezra or some other biblical figure is certainly possible, but since I have not investigated the issue of authorship, I have decided to use the anonymous label. Using "Chronicler" is thus not an attack on the traditional view of authorship. It is a confession of ignorance.

[3] Several articles offer helpful commentary on the structure and themes of this section of Chronicles. William Johnstone, "Guilt and Atonement: The Theme of 1 and 2 Chronicles," in James D. Martin and Philip R. Davies, eds., *A Word in Season: Essays in Honour of William McKane* (*JSOT* Supplement #42; Sheffield: Sheffield Academic Press, 1986), 113–138, is a superb, even electrifying, discussion of the themes of sacrilege (Heb. *ma'al*), exile, and redemption in Chronicles. See also Tamara C. Eskenazi, "A Literary Approach to Chronicles' Ark Narrative in 1 Chronicles 13–16," in Astrid B. Beck, et. al., eds., *Fortunate the Eyes that See: Essays in Honor of David N. Freedman* (Grand Rapids: Eerdmans, 1995), 258–273; Simon J. DeVries, "Moses and David as Cult Founders in Chronicles," *Journal of Biblical Literature* 107, no. 4 (1988): 619–639; and John W. Wright, "The Founding Father: The Structure of the Chronicler's David Narrative," *Journal of Biblical Literature* 117, no. 1 (1998): 45–59. Wright has also dealt with some of the surrounding chapters in several articles: "Guarding the Gates: 1 Chronicles 26:1–19 and the Roles of Gatekeepers in Chronicles," *Journal for the Study of the Old Testament* 48 (1990): 69–81, and "The Legacy of David in Chronicles: The Narrative Function of 1 Chronicles 23–27," *Journal of Biblical Literature* 110, no. 2 (1991): 229–242.

bosheth, whereas several chapters of 2 Samuel describe this struggle (chapters 2–4). 1 Chronicles moves directly from the death of Saul (chapter 10) to the gathering of Israel at Hebron to anoint David king over all the tribes (chapters 11–12). More generally, the seven years of David's reign in Hebron over the tribe of Judah are virtually bypassed.[4] Instead of recounting a contested succession, the Chronicler writes simply that Yahweh "killed" Saul "and turned the kingdom to David the son of Jesse" (10:14).

Second, 1 Chronicles devotes a great deal more attention to the ceremony of David's coronation at Hebron than Samuel. 2 Samuel describes the event in five terse verses (5:1–5), but 1 Chronicles spends two entire chapters (11–12) on the event. These chapters record other incidents and information as well: the conquest of Jerusalem (11:4–9; compare 2 Sam. 5:6–10), a list of David's mighty men (11:10–47; compare 2 Sam. 23:8–39), and a list of the men who came to David in Ziklag (12:1–22; no parallel in 2 Sam.). Yet the chapters are a single unit, framed by an *inclusio* concerning the coronation ceremony at Hebron:

> So all the elders of Israel came to the king at Hebron, and David made a covenant with them in Hebron before Yahweh; and they *anointed David king* over Israel, according to the word of Yahweh through Samuel. (11:3)

> All these, being men of war, who could draw up in battle formation, came to David with a perfect heart, *to make David king* over all Israel; and all the rest also of Israel were of one mind *to make David king*. (12:38)

What seems a fairly low-key affair in 2 Samuel 5 becomes a tremendous ceremony in 1 Chronicles, attended by more than 300,000 fighting men from every tribe (12:23–37).

Another change has to do with the order of events between David's coronation as king over all Israel and the ascension of the ark to Jerusalem. The sequence in 2 Samuel is as follows:

---

[4] To be sure, Hebron is mentioned as David's residence in 1 Chronicles 11:1, and even David's sojourn in Ziklag is alluded to (12:1). But Chronicles does not mention the fact that David reigned only over Judah for a time or that he fled to Ziklag to escape from Saul.

Conquest of Jerusalem, 5:6–10
David's palace and family, 5:11–16
Two battles with the Philistines, 5:17–25
The ark taken to Zion (failed first attempt), 6:1–11
The ark taken to Zion (successful second attempt), 6:12–19
Michal's complaint against David, 6:20–23
The Davidic covenant, 7:1–29

1 Chronicles 13–16 records the same events in a different order:

First attempt to bring the ark to Jerusalem, 13:1–14[5]
David's palace and family, 14:1–7
Two battles with the Philistines, 14:8–17
Second attempt to bring ark to Jerusalem, 15:1–16:43[6]
The Davidic covenant, 17:1–27

Though the order is different in Chronicles, the "victory-housebuilding" pattern is still evident. Only after Yahweh has defeated the Philistines does His throne ascend to Zion. In addition, Chronicles includes a great deal more information about the procession of the ark and its establishment in the Zion tent. Levites are listed at length (15:1–24; 16:4–6, 37–38), and the role of music in Davidic worship, which is not even mentioned in 2 Samuel, is emphasized.

Several effects of these changes may be noted. First, the Chronicler presents a more uniformly positive picture of David than 2 Samuel does. Though 2 Samuel's portrayal is generally favorable, the author records David's sins without flinching. The more positive presentation in Chronicles is evident even in some subtle details of

[5] David's conquest of Jerusalem is described in 11:4–7, within the chapters that describe the coronation of David over Israel.

[6] Chapters 15–16 form a single unit of text. Chapter 15 opens with David giving instructions to the Levites concerning the portage of the ark (15:1–15), and chapter 16 ends with the assignment of duties to the Levites and priests at the two sanctuaries in Zion and Gibeon (16:37–43). Further, the passage begins with a gathering of Israel (15:3), and ends with their dispersal (16:43).

the Chronicler's treatment. For example, the list of mighty men in 2 Samuel 23 ends with "Uriah the Hittite," a powerful reminder of David's sin with Bathsheba that provides an introduction to the story of David's further sin in the following chapter. By contrast, in the similar record of mighty men in 1 Chronicles 11, Uriah's name is buried in the middle of the list (v. 41), with no special attention paid to him. Similarly, 1 Chronicles 20 begins with an almost verbatim repetition of 2 Samuel 11: "Then it happened in the spring, at the time when kings go out" (2 Sam. 11:1; 1 Chr. 20:1). 2 Samuel 11:1 ends with the statement that "David stayed at Jerusalem," and the remainder of chapter 11 and much of chapter 12 record the story of David's adultery and murder. 1 Chronicles 20:1 adds the sentence: "And David struck Rabbah and overthrew it," which is similar to the statement in 2 Samuel 12:26, *after* David's sin. In a single verse—1 Chronicles 20:1—the Chronicler skips from the opening of 2 Samuel 11 to the end of 2 Samuel 12. That is to say, he ignores the whole story of Bathsheba and Uriah.[7]

Another effect of these changes is to shift the emphasis of David's reign. In 2 Samuel, David is in the main a great warrior-king. Prior to his sin with Bathsheba, 2 Samuel records his victory over Ishbosheth, his conquest of Jerusalem, two victories over the Philistines, and his triumphs in assorted wars with the Moabites, Ammonites, Arameans, and others (2 Sam. 2–5, 8). Much of this material is repeated in Chronicles, but the Chronicler embeds David's life as a warrior in descriptions of David's other activities, and as a result David as warrior-king takes a secondary position to his other roles. In particular, what comes to the foreground are David's efforts to prepare for the eventual building of the temple.

[7] This might seem like a thorough white–washing, but it is not. Though the Chronicler does not mention Bathsheba, he was writing to a post-exilic Israel that had had the book of Samuel for several centuries. It was too late to clean up David's reputation, if that was the intention. Had the Chronicler intended this, furthermore, he could have told the story in a way that shifted blame to someone else, rather than simply ignore the incident. Bill Clinton's defenders are not content to pass over Monicagate in silence; they offer an alternative account that blames elderly Republican women who own copier machines and know how to send email—that is, the vast right-wing conspiracy.

2 Samuel includes virtually no information about this. 2 Samuel 8:11 tells us that David dedicated the spoils of war to the Lord, but it is not even clear in that passage how the dedicated spoils were to be used. In Chronicles, David, even more than Solomon, is presented as the temple-builder, the one who founded the worship of Israel in Jerusalem. David organized the Levites and priests for musical ministry at the tabernacle of David (1 Chr. 15–16), reassigned Levites to ministry at the temple that Solomon would build (1 Chr. 23–27), delivered the plans for the temple to Solomon (1 Chr. 28:19), and gathered, protected, and inventoried materials and builders for the temple (1 Chr. 22:14–16; 29:1–5).[8]

This emphasis is apparent when we compare the Chronicler's account of an event of David's reign with that of Samuel. Both 1 Chronicles 21 and 2 Samuel 24 tell about David's purchase of the threshing floor of Araunah the Jebusite. This location becomes the temple site, but we never learn that in 2 Samuel. That information comes in 2 Chronicles 3:1. Further, 1 Chronicles 21 includes details that are not found in 2 Samuel 24. When David built the altar

---

[8] To be sure, David's organization of Israel is political as well as liturgical, as John W. Wright has pointed out ("The Founding Father," esp. 49, 59), but Wright is being wholly modern when he sets David's work as "the founding father of the Israelite/Judean state" over against his role as "merely the initiator of true worship in Israel" (49). Building the temple was a political act and David's goal was to organize the kingdom over which Yahweh ruled; politics and worship may be distinguishable, but they could not be separated in ancient Israel. Moreover, Wright himself provides evidence that the Chronicler placed the ministry of the Levites at the center of David's organization of the *political* system. As he points out, 1 Chronicles 23:1–2 lists three leaders of the future: Solomon, "the leaders of Israel," and "the priests and Levites." Over the following chapters, David organizes/instructs each of these in reverse order:
   Levites, 23:2–26:32
   Civil leaders, 27:1–34
   Exhortation to Solomon, 28:1–29:30
Thus, the structure of chapters 23–29 is as follows:
   Solomon made king
   Civil leaders gathered
   Priests and Levites gathered
   Priests and Levites organized
   Civil leaders organized
   Solomon exhorted
Even on Wright's evidence, then, the priests and Levites are structurally central to what he describes as the "political" organization in chapters 23–29.

on the threshing floor and called on Yahweh, "He answered him with fire from heaven on the altar of burnt offering" (1 Chr. 21:26). This scene does not appear in 2 Samuel 24; instead, it is reminiscent of Leviticus 9:24, when the Lord's fire consumed the sacrificial portions on the altar at the end of the rite dedicating the Mosaic tabernacle and consecrating Aaron and his sons as priests. In Leviticus, this is the sign that Yahweh has taken up residence in His house and has accepted Aaron's offerings, and David got the same message when the Lord's fire consumed his offering at the threshing floor of Araunah. David recognized that Yahweh's fire had designated this location as the place where He would dwell, and said, in a statement not found in 2 Samuel, "This is the house of Yahweh God, and this is the altar of burnt offering for Israel" (1 Chr. 22:1). Through this event, David recognized that Yahweh had authorized *sacrificial* worship in Jerusalem, on Mount Moriah. Thus, what 2 Samuel 24 presents mainly as a real estate transaction becomes a temple-founding in 1 Chronicles 21.[9]

Given this background, it is no surprise that the Chronicler describes Solomon's temple-building as a completion of the work that David had begun. Solomon built the temple "where the Lord had appeared to his father David, at the place that David had prepared" (2 Chr. 3:1). Temple utensils are described as "dedicated things of David his father, even the silver and the gold and all the utensils" (2 Chr. 5:1), and the temple fulfills the promises of Yahweh to David (2 Chr. 6:4–6). For the Chronicler, David was not so much a warrior as a worshiper, not so much hero as hierophant.

## David, the New Moses

Consistent with this overall liturgical interest, Chronicles presents David as a new Moses, who, with the great prophet, co-founded the worship of Israel.[10] The simple fact that Chronicles devotes so much

[9] For further discussion of the significance of 2 Samuel 24 in the light of Abraham's purchase of Machpelah in Genesis 23, see my *A Son to Me*.

[10] See especially De Vries, "Moses and David as Cult Founders."

space to David's preparations for the temple is enough to bring out parallels with Moses, since much of the revelation given to Moses concerned the tabernacle, its furnishings, and its worship (Exod. 25–31, 35–40; Leviticus; Num. 3–9). Like Moses, David assigned duties to the priests and Levites. Like Moses, David received a "pattern" for the house of Yahweh (Exod. 25:9, 40; 26:30; 1 Chr. 28:19). Like Moses, David ensured that the plundered riches of Yahweh's enemies were devoted to the service of His house.

The Chronicler also appeals to the commands and ordinances of David as authoritative instruction for Israel's worship.[11] This is not to say that Chronicles subverts the liturgical authority of Moses; as the repetition of the phrase "as Moses commanded" indicates, the Mosaic ceremonial laws remained authoritative for Israel throughout the period of the monarchy (1 Chr. 6:49; 15:15; 2 Chr. 8:12–13; 23:18; 24:6, 9; 35:6). Alongside these references to Moses, however, the Chronicler also refers with some frequency to the liturgical authority of David. In 2 Chronicles 8:13–14, David's "ordinance" concerning the "divisions of priests for their service, and the Levites for their duties" is set alongside "the commandment of Moses" concerning the festival calendar of Israel.[12] Similarly, 2 Chronicles 23:18 records that "Jehoiada placed the offices of the house of the Lord under the authority of the Levitical priests, whom David had assigned over the house of Yahweh, to offer the ascension offerings of Yahweh, as it is written in the law of Moses."

When Josiah celebrated the Passover, he instructed the Levites to "prepare yourselves by your fathers' households in your divisions, according to the writing of David king of Israel and according to the writing of his son Solomon" (2 Chr. 35:4). The Levitical musicians at Josiah's Passover "were also at their stations according to the command of David, Asaph, Heman, and Jeduthun the king's seer" (2 Chr. 35:15).

---

[11] Ibid. Also John W. Kleinig, *The Lord's Song: The Basis, Function, and Significance of Choral Music in Chronicles* (*JSOT* Supplement #156; Sheffield: *JSOT* Press, 1993), 28–29.

[12] Significantly, David is given the Mosaic title "man of God" in 2 Chronicles 8:14.

If David was a new Moses, Solomon was a new Joshua, whose temple-building is implicitly compared to the conquest.[13] David's frequent encouragement to Solomon to "be strong and courageous" (1 Chr. 22:13; 28:10, 20), echoes Moses' instructions to Joshua, his successor (see Josh. 1:7, 9, 18; Deut 31:6–7, 23).[14] As Joshua was to cling to the word of the Lord delivered through Moses (Josh. 1:7–8), so Solomon was to walk in the way of the Lord's commandments "as your father David walked" (1 Kgs. 3:14; 9:4).

The notion that David is a new Moses, founding a new "cult," helps to explain some of the peculiarities of the tabernacle of David. After the exodus, Moses pitched a tent outside the camp (Exod. 33:7–11) and later organized the building of the tabernacle and turned its care over to the priests. Similarly, after David's exodus from Philistia, he erected a tent on Zion and then organized the building of a temple, which was eventually turned over to the care of priests. And, just as Moses had direct access to Yahweh in the tent of meeting, so David had direct access to Yahweh in the tent on Zion (see chapter 3 below). The parallels between David and Moses are not exact, but in each case, the sanctuary was established in two stages, a sequence repeated in the post-exilic period, for the altar was restored some twenty years before the temple was completed (Ezra 3:1–6; 4:24; 6:13–18). As we shall see, this sequence of sanctuaries came to ultimate fruition in the new covenant.

## The Song at the Center of the World

Though the Chronicler's account of David's reign begins in chapter 11, the main themes have already been signaled in the first ten chapters of the book, and these chapters help to specify the focal point of the Chronicler's liturgical interests. Famously, Chronicles

---

[13] See Wright, "The Founding Father," 57.

[14] The reasons for David's exhortations are not clear: What threat did Solomon face that demanded courage? In part, this exhortation highlights the fact that the temple was the conclusion and final act of the conquest. But the exhortations are most directly relevant to the original post-exilic readers of Chronicles, for, unlike Solomon, they rebuilt the temple under threat from the surrounding nations.

begins with nine chapters of mainly genealogical information (plus a mantra thrown in for good measure). Though these chapters are sometimes little more than lists, a number of key theological issues are introduced. The first half of chapter 1 is devoted to the generations between Adam and Abraham (1:1–27), which, as William Johnstone has pointed out, sets "the descendants of Abraham within the context of the whole family of mankind." Moreover, the brief narrative fragments in this genealogy highlight the fact that man's history "is characterized from the beginning by a pattern of false starts and abortive restarts." Nimrod, "the mighty one in the earth" (v. 10), represents the violence that spread throughout the world, while the Chronicler's reference to the division of the earth (v. 19) reminds us of the conflicts among nations after the flood. Before Israel is introduced into the Chronicler's history, then, some of the central effects of sin have been identified. In this context Israel's calling is made clear: "Israel is to realize on behalf of mankind what mankind as a whole cannot."[15]

The arrangement of the tribal genealogies of Israel, furthermore, shows *how* Israel was to address evils that characterize the Gentile world. James B. Jordan has suggested that the genealogies as a whole are arranged chiastically:

A. Roots of Israel, 1:1–2:2
   B. Judah: Royal tribe, 2:3–4:23 (Simeon attached, 4:23–43)
      C. Transjordan tribes (east of the Jordan River), ch. 5
         D. Levi, ch. 6
      C'. Cisjordan tribes (west of the Jordan river), ch. 7
   B'. Benjamin: Royal tribe, ch. 8
A'. Jerusalem, 9:1–34
   1. Judah, vv. 3–6
   2. Benjamin, vv. 7–9

---

[15] Johnstone, "Guilt and Atonement," 126–127. Of course, Chronicles as a whole shows that Israel too fails in this task. It will take a new Israel to fulfill Israel's calling, and that new Israel is named Jesus.

3. Priests, vv. 10–13
4. Levites, vv. 14–34[16]

The position of the Levites is particularly noteworthy here: They are central to the structure, the hinge on which the world-genealogy turns, and Levites reappear at the climax of the genealogies. Adam's race, as it were, comes most fully to itself in the ministry of the Levites in Jerusalem. Worship is the goal of humanity, and worship is also the means by which Israel is to realize her mission among the nations.

Structurally, the emphasis on the Levites is specified further, for the genealogy of Levi in chapter 6 is itself arranged chiastically:

A. Priests, 6:1–16
  B. Levites, 6:17–30
    C. Levitical Musicians, 6:31–47
  B'. Levitical ministry in general, 6:48
A'. Priestly line, 6:49–53[17]

Thus, the central section of the Chronicler's genealogical summary of world history lists Levites "whom David appointed over the service of song in the house of Yahweh, after the ark rested" (6:31). Not worship in general, but specifically *musical* worship, worship in song, is the Chronicler's central concern. In the context of the genealogies, the focus on Levitical song is making a large point about

[16] James B. Jordan, "1 Chronicles and Levites" (Lecture Notes to the Eleventh Annual Biblical Horizons Summer Conference, 2001), 12. Tapes and notes are available from Biblical Horizons, P.O. Box 1096, Niceville, Florida, 32588. Johnstone, similarly, concludes that the genealogies of Israel are arranged chiastically, with Levi at the center:
  A. Southern tribes: Judah and Simeon
    B. Northern tribes: Reuben, Gad, Half-Manasseh
      C. Levi
    B'. Northern tribes: Issachar, Benjamin, Naphtali, Half-Manasseh, Ephraim, Asher
  A'. Southern tribe: Benjamin
See "Guilt and Atonement," 128.
[17] This outline is a slightly modified version of Jordan's outline in "1 Chronicles and Levites," 14. The remainder of chapter 6 lists the cities of the Levites according to Levitical clans.

the role of music in human history: Adam's race is created for song, destined to become a great Levitical chorus. And, song is the means (or, one of the means) by which Adam's race will reach this end. In this way, the genealogies anticipate the emphasis on music that is found throughout the remainder of Chronicles, and in the account of David's reign in particular. Under David, and at the Davidic tabernacle, Israel begins to sing the eschatological song of the race of the new Adam.

Why that song begins in David's reign will become apparent when the "eschatological" features of the Davidic tent have been explored, an expedition undertaken in the next chapter.

# 3
# Some for Priests and Levites

When David brought the ark into Jerusalem, he set it in the "place" that he had "prepared" for it. The word "place" (*maqom*), used in both 2 Samuel 6:17 and 1 Chronicles 15:1, reverberates momentously. It appears throughout Deuteronomy 12 to refer to the "place" where the Lord's name would dwell after He brought rest to Israel (vv. 3, 5, 11, 13–14, 18, 21, 26) and occurs in other passages of Deuteronomy to describe the "place" where feasts were celebrated (14:23–24; 16:6, 11, 15). It connotes a fixed location for the Lord's dwelling, in opposition to the mobile and temporary placements of the Mosaic tabernacle. Apart from these passages of Deuteronomy, the word is not frequently used in the Pentateuch, for so long as Israel was in the wilderness, the sanctuary was not in a "place" but something traveling from "place to place."

When 2 Samuel 6:17 and 1 Chronicles 15:1 describe the location of David's tent with this word, then, two things are being said. First, the ascension of the ark to Zion fulfills the promise of Deuteronomy 12. When Yahweh's throne is placed in David's tent, it means that Yahweh has chosen a "place" and set His name there. And second, this "place" is the permanent, fixed location for the Lord's house; the ark has been "placed" in its "place" and will no more move from "place to place." Once He rests on Zion, Yahweh will not again move (Ps. 132:13–14). The allusion to Deuteronomy, then, suggests that the ascension of the ark marked an endpoint in the story of the ark. The procession to Zion was an "eschaton." No wonder David was so jazzed.

"An" end, but not "the" end, for the ark did in fact move again, into the temple of Solomon, another "place" prepared for it (2 Chr. 3:1; 5:2–10). In the story of the ark, in short, we find a double eschaton; when the ark came to Zion, the end had already come, but at the same time the end had not yet come. Yet, the fact that Zion is "an" end rather than "the" end does not cancel the eschatological significance of David's tent. It was not so much that the ark moved from the place at Zion to another place at Moriah. It was rather that "Zion" was moved to "Moriah," as the ark-tent incorporated into the more glorious temple. Yahweh did not move from His place, but took His place with Him.

The allusion to Deuteronomy thus supports Tamara Eskenazi's comment that the ascension of the ark to Zion was an event of "global" and "cosmic" magnitude. And many of the features of the Davidic tent underline these dimensions. As we shall see in this chapter, the tabernacle of David was an historical prototype of crucial features of New Covenant worship.

### The First Tent

Architecturally, the Davidic tent was radically different from the Mosaic. Moses' tabernacle was divided into three areas, the courtyard, Holy Place, and Most Holy Place, and each "room" housed particular pieces of furniture. David's tent, by contrast, contained only the ark and, though Scripture provides no floor plan, several lines of evidence indicate that it was an undivided tent. As we shall see, these architectural features—the fact that David's tent was a single room containing a single piece of furniture—offer an important clue to its theological significance.

How do we know that David's tent was a single room with a single piece of furniture? In part the evidence is negative: Scripture never mentions distinct rooms within the shrine and speaks only of the ark being placed there (2 Sam. 6:17; 1 Chr. 15:1). But there is also positive evidence. It is especially clear that the only major piece of furniture was the ark, the throne of Yahweh, where He sat over the outstretched wings of the cherubim. 1 Chronicles 16:39–40 informs us that David left the Zadokite priests in charge of the Mosaic "tabernacle of Yahweh in the high place which was at Gibeon, to offer ascensions to Yahweh on the altar of ascensions continually morning and evening, even according to all that is written in the law of Yahweh, which He commanded Israel." If the Mosaic tabernacle was at Gibeon, and not at Zion, that means that the rest of the furniture of the Mosaic tabernacle (the laver, the table of showbread, the lampstand, and the altar of incense) was also at Gibeon. Unless David constructed another piece of sanctuary furniture—and there is no record that he did so—the only item that was not in Gibeon was the ark.

One passage indicates that there were other "utensils" (*keli*) at the ark-tent on Zion. When Solomon brought the ark from Zion to Moriah, he brought "all the holy utensils" with it (2 Chr. 5:5), but these implements are not listed or described. By the time the ark was set in the temple, the house was already furnished with an altar, the bronze sea, ten water basins, as well as "the golden altar, the tables with Bread of the Presence on them, the lampstands with their lamps of pure gold . . . the flowers, the lamps, and the tongs of gold, of purest gold; and the snuffers, the bowls, the spoons, and the firepans of pure gold" (2 Chr. 4:1–22). It is possible that "holy utensils" in 2 Chronicles 5:5 refers to musical instruments; as we shall see in chapter 4, the same Hebrew word is used for both musical instruments and sacrificial tools like snuffers, shovels, and forks. But whatever the "holy utensils" were, however, they were not the large objects described in Exodus 25–40, since those were already in the temple before the ark arrived. That means that the ark was the only piece of furniture in David's tent.

And this, in turn, confirms that the tent was a single room. The whole Mosaic tabernacle system was organized according to a pattern of "graded holiness."[1] Different spaces within the tabernacle possessed different intensities of holiness because they were at varying distances from the Lord's presence. Moreover, the value of the furniture in each room corresponded to the degree of holiness. The bronze altar was less valuable than the golden altar of incense, and the latter, made of wood overlaid with gold, was of lesser value than the ark with its cover and cherubim of pure gold. Gradation of value matched the gradation of holiness; Israelite laymen were not allowed to touch or approach the bronze altar, but they never even *saw* the golden altar, which was in the Holy Place where only priests ministered. And not even the priests saw or approached the ark.[2] Since David's ark-shrine contained no other furnishings than the ark, there was obviously no gradation of furniture, and this implies that there was not a graded spatial arrangement either. There was no other furniture of lesser (or greater) value, and therefore no space of lesser (or greater) holiness, no distinction of "holy space" and "most holy space."

The fact that the Davidic tabernacle was undivided is one of its most striking features. According to Hebrews 9, the division of the Mosaic tabernacle into a "first tent" (the Holy Place, v. 2) and "second tent" (the Most Holy Place, vv. 3–5) was an architectural parable concerning the condition of Israel under the Old Covenant:

> The Holy Spirit is signifying this, that the way into the holy place had not yet been disclosed, while the first tent is still standing, which is a symbol for the present time. Accordingly both gifts and sacrifices are offered which cannot make the worshiper perfect in conscience, since they relate only to food and drink and various washings, regulations for the flesh imposed until a time of reformation. (Heb. 9:8–10)

---

[1] For an excellent overview of the Mosaic system, see Philip Peter Jenson, *Graded Holiness: A Key to the Priestly Conception of the World* (Sheffield: Sheffield Academic Press, 1992).

[2] For further discussion, see Menahem Haran, *Temples and Temple-Service in Ancient Israel: An Inquiry into Biblical Cult Phenomena and the Historical Setting of the Priestly School* (Winona Lake, Ind.: Eisenbrauns, 1985), 158–165; James B. Jordan, "From Glory to Glory: Degrees of Value in the Sanctuary," Biblical Horizons Occasional Paper, available from Biblical Horizons, P.O. Box 1096, Niceville, FL 32588.

The existence of a "first tent" in the Mosaic sanctuary thus points to the fact that Israel was excluded from the presence of God. In fact, the existence of the first tent enforced this exclusion, since God's glory was hidden in an inner room of the tabernacle, separated from the people by sheer physical space of the first tent. Conversely, the fact that David's tent was undivided and did not have a "first tent" suggests that "the way into the holy place" *had* been disclosed in David's time. David's tent points ahead to the undivided sanctuary of his Greater Son, whose death rent the veil that separated the temple and disclosed the way into the holy place.

*Before the Ark*

Reasoning with the author of Hebrews, we would anticipate that David's tent would offer nearer access to Yahweh than the tabernacle of Moses. Our anticipation does not go unsatisfied. A number of places in 1 Chronicles describe the location of the Levitical ministers:

> [David] appointed some of the Levites as ministers *before the ark of Yahweh*. (1 Chr. 16:4)

> Benaiah and Jahaziel the priests blew trumpets continually *before the ark of the covenant of God.* (1 Chr. 16:6)

> [David] left Asaph and his brothers there *before the ark of the covenant of Yahweh*, to minister *before the ark* continually, as each day's work required. (1 Chr. 16:37)

Surprisingly, this phrase is never used of priestly or Levitical ministry in the Mosaic law. The phrase "before the ark" occurs in Exodus 40:5, but refers there to the placement of the golden altar of incense in the Holy Place. Even Leviticus 16, which describes the Day of Atonement when the High Priest entered the Most Holy Place to sprinkle blood, does not say that the priest entered "before the ark." The chapter mentions the ark only once (v. 2), and says that the High Priest ministered "before the cover that is on the ark" (v.

2) and sprinkled blood "on the cover on the east side, also in front of the cover" (v. 14). Even when the High Priest got as close as he ever got to the Lord's throne, he was not described as ministering "before the ark." And nobody, of course, ever got any closer than the High Priest. Significantly, when 1 Chronicles 25 describes the ministry of Levitical singers and musicians in the *temple*, it does not use the phrase "before the ark." Rather, the Levites were appointed to sing "in the house of Yahweh" (v. 6). At David's tent, however, lowly Levites ministered "before the ark." This location was unique to David's tent; never before and never again would Old Covenant Israel be privileged to worship "before the ark."[3]

Not only the Levites, but David too had remarkably free access to the tent and the ark within. After the ark had been placed in Zion, David intended to build a temple as a permanent house for Yahweh, but through Nathan the Lord informed him that his son would complete that project. After hearing the promises of God through Nathan, David "went in and sat before the Lord" (2 Sam. 7:18; 1 Chr. 17:16). Where did he go? Evidently, he was indoors somewhere, and that place was "before Yahweh." The most obvious place to sit "before Yahweh" was within the tent, before the ark.

This is confirmed by the use of phrases like "before Yahweh" in the surrounding context of 1 Chronicles. As the ark is brought to Jerusalem, "David and all Israel were celebrating before God" (13:8), which means "before the ark." When Uzzah touched the ark, he "died there before God" (13:10), again, literally, before the ark. Offering burnt offerings and peace offerings at the ark-shrine in Zion is described as offering them "before God" (16:1). Thus, when David went in "before God," he went into the tent and sat down before Yahweh's throne. Later, Solomon's palace was incorporated

---

[3] It is not clear precisely where the Levites were stationed in relation to the Davidic tent. Perhaps they performed their ministry outside the tent, but this was close enough to be described as "before the ark." Alternatively, it is possible that the tent was large enough to accommodate Levites within, so that they offered worship literally "before the ark." Since the law governing the sight of the ark had not been changed, however, it is certain that the ark was covered during the time it was stationed at Zion. Though the Levites performed before the ark, they never saw the ark. Wonderful though it was, the Davidic covenant was still part of the old creation.

into the temple-complex, a permanent symbol of the privileged position of the Davidic king. The ark-shrine was thus not only a sign of Yahweh's access, but also symbolized the position of the Davidic king. As a new Moses, David could enter before Yahweh and speak "face to face" with Him; as a new Adam, the "son" of Yahweh, David could enter to speak with his Father; as the anointed of the Lord, David could even take a seat, enthroned at his Father's right hand.

Kevin Conner has argued that there were in fact two tents of David.[4] Conner calls the ark-shrine the "Davidic worship tabernacle," but in addition he speaks of a "Davidic kingdom tabernacle" in which David was enthroned as judge and civil ruler. There is a liturgical tent and a political tent. As support for this conception, Conner cites Isaiah 16:5: "A throne will even be established in lovingkindness, and a judge will sit on it in faithfulness in the tent of David; moreover, he will seek justice and be prompt in righteousness." Conner argues that Isaiah was prophesying about the restoration of the "Davidic kingdom tabernacle," that is, of Davidic political order, but not directly speaking of the restoration of Davidic liturgy. The fact that David could "go in and sit before Yahweh" in the ark-shrine, however, shows that Conner's thesis of a double-tent is unnecessary. The "worship tabernacle" was at the same time the tent where David was enthroned as Yahweh's deputy. Promises of the restoration of David's kingdom include the promise of a restored Davidic worship, and promises of the restoration of Davidic worship include the promise of a revived Davidic kingdom.

## Let All the Peoples Praise Thee

David's enthronement in the tent on Zion at the right hand of the High King demonstrated Yahweh's favor to him, and his high

---

[4] Conner, *The Tabernacle of David* (Portland, Ore.: Bible Temple-Conner Publications, 1976), chap. 7. It is not clear whether Conner is simply arguing that the phrase "tent of David" can have two distinct senses, or if he believes that there were in fact two distinct tents. Since some of his formulations suggest the latter, I have taken that as his position.

position in Israel. But David was also being exalted over the nations. According to the account in 2 Samuel, he had already conquered the Jebusites and Philistines before bringing the ark to Jerusalem, and 1 Chronicles, importantly, places the Philistine wars between David's first and second attempts to transfer the ark (14:8–17). Thus, in 1 Chronicles, we have this sequence: first, there is an unsuccessful attempt to bring Yahweh's throne to Jerusalem; then David fights and defeats the Philistines; then Yahweh's throne ascends to Zion; and a few chapters later, David sat "before Yahweh." The Chronicler does not leave the import of this to our imagination; he tells us, after recording David's victories over the Philistines, that "the fame of David went out into all the lands; and Yahweh brought the fear of him on all the nations" (14:17). The ark-tent on Zion symbolizes the international status of Yahweh, and of David.

The architecture of the Davidic tent, discussed above, is again relevant. Among other things, the graded holiness of the Mosaic tabernacle—its division into courtyard, Holy Place, and Most Holy Place—represented the holiness distinctions among different groups of people in the Old Covenant. It was a spatial symbol of the division of Israel into High Priest, priests, and people, and also highlighted the division between Israel and the Gentiles. Though Gentiles could sacrifice in the tabernacle courtyard (Num. 15:11–16), the system as a whole represented the division of Jew and Gentile. By contrast, the fact that David's tent was undivided suggests that it would be more amenable to Gentile participation. The removal of the dividing veil not only meant greater access to Yahweh's presence, but also access for different sorts of people. The architecture of David's tent leads us to anticipate that Gentiles will be included in Israel's worship as never before.

Again, our anticipation is satisfied. Gentiles began ministering to Yahweh even before David's day. Before the ark came to Zion, it spent a century in the house of a Gentile. When the Philistines returned the ark to Israel after holding it for seven months, they sent it to Beth-shemesh (1 Sam. 6:10–12), a Levitical city belonging to the family of Aaron (Josh. 21:16). The Levites of Beth-shemesh looked "at" or "into" the ark, and Yahweh judged this violation of the law (see Num. 4:19–20) by sending a plague that killed 50,070 men (1 Sam. 6:10–21). Just as the Lord had plagued the Philistines for their abuse of his throne, so He plagued Israelites who acted no better than Philistines. Instead of repenting, however, the Levites of Beth-shemesh sent the ark away, just as the Philistines had done.

The ark ended up at Kiriath-jearim, one of the cities of the Gibeonites (Josh. 9:17). Gibeonites were a Canaanite (Hivite) people who deceived Israel into agreeing to a covenant in the days of Joshua. When Joshua discovered who the Gibeonites really were, he insisted that the covenant was inviolable, since it had been sworn in the holy name of Yahweh. Thus, the Gibeonites were not destroyed but were incorporated into Israel as servants at the tabernacle, hewing wood and drawing water for the work of the altar (Josh. 9:27). Kiriath-jearim in particular was in the tribal territory of Judah or Benjamin (Josh. 15:9, 60), and the fact that one of Caleb's descendants was identified as the "father of Kiriath-jearim" (1 Chr. 2:50, 52) suggests that the city was in the area populated by the Calebite clan. Yet, the city remained largely Gentile and certainly was a Gentile city in origin. Of course, Gibeonites had worked at the altar before, but had never cared for the ark. In fact, no Gentile had ever cared for the ark, apart from the Philistines, yet they mucked up the job pretty badly. How would the Gibeonites of Kiriath-jearim do?

Specifically, the ark was placed in the house of Abinadab on the hill (1 Sam. 7:1–2), who was almost certainly a Gentile himself. A few Israelites named Abinadab are mentioned in the Old Testament. David had a brother named Abinadab (1 Sam. 16:8), and Saul had a son of the same name (1 Sam. 31:2), but nothing explicitly connects Abinadab of Kiriath-jearim with either of these men, and the evidence is against any such identification. If Abinadab of Kiriath-jearim had close family connections with one of the first two kings of Israel, it is odd that the Bible never mentions it. Further, his sons (or descendants), Uzzah and Ahio (2 Sam. 6:3), are not found in the genealogies of Israel in Chronicles. An Uzzah appears in the genealogy of Levi (1 Chr. 6:29) and a Benjamite "Uzza" is found in 1 Chronicles 8:7, but neither is connected to anyone called Abinadab. Given the fact that the ark remained in Abinadab's house for a century, the absence of his family from the genealogies is striking. Abinadab of Kiriath-jearim is never identified as an Israelite in any text of the Old Testament, and his residence in a Gibeonite city identifies him as a Gentile.

Lacking explicit information about Abinadab's ethnic origins, our conclusion that he was a Gentile is necessarily somewhat tentative. Even if he was an Israelite, however, we can be sure that he was not a Levite. According to David's statement in 1 Chronicles 15:2, one of David's errors in his first attempt to bring the ark into Jerusalem was his failure to assign Levites the task of carrying the ark. Yahweh had explicitly commanded that "no one is to carry the ark of God but the Levites," but the first time David tried to bring the ark to Jerusalem "you [i.e., the Levites] did not carry it" (1 Chr. 15:13). In the first effort to bring the ark to Jerusalem, it was carried by Uzzah and Ahio, sons of Abinadab (2 Sam. 6:3). David thus made it explicit that Abinadab's sons were not Levites, and therefore Abinadab was not a Levite either.

Though the Law assigned the task of guarding the ark to Levites and priests, however, the ark was left in the care of Abinadab, a non-Levite and probably a non-Israelite. Certainly, the ark was housed during this period in a Gentile city, for even in David's day the Gibeonites were separate from Israel: "the Gibeonites were not of the sons of Israel but of the remnant of the Amorites" (2 Sam. 21:2). During this period, there is no evidence that Yahweh was displeased that His ark remained in a Gentile city cared for by non-Levites (probably Gentiles), nor is there evidence that Samuel or anyone else made any effort to bring the ark from Kiriath-jearim. This period witnessed unprecedented participation of non-Levites in ministry to Yahweh and His throne.

*Another Philistine Exile*

Increased Gentile participation continued after David brought the ark to Jerusalem. The first attempt to bring the ark to Zion ended abruptly when Uzzah touched the ark and was killed. A fresh corpse will put a damper on the celebration every time. Naturally fearful of bringing the ark to Zion, David sent it to the home of one "Obed-edom," a "Gittite" (2 Sam. 6:10; 1 Chr. 13:13), and several pieces of evidence make it certain that Obed-edom was a Gentile. Start with his name, which means "servant of Edom," unimaginable for an Israelite. Further, he is called a "Gittite," and everywhere else this word is used it refers to a resident of the Philistine city of Gath. Joshua 13:3 includes the "Gittites" among the heads of the Philistine cities. The commander of David's bodyguard was "Ittai the Gittite" (2 Sam. 15:18–19; 18:2), and he headed a company of Gentile mercenaries who had attached themselves to David. Goliath is called a Gittite (2 Sam. 21:19; 1 Chr. 20:5), and is elsewhere known as the Philistine giant of Gath (1 Sam. 17:4).

To be sure, other city names are compounds with "Gath," and one of them, Gath-rimmon, was a Levitical city (Josh. 19:45; 21:24–25; 1 Chr. 6:69). Yet this obscure city is found only in lists of Levitical cities and plays no role whatever in the history of David. Referring to a resident of that city as a "Gittite" without further specification invites confusion. Besides, the Old Testament does not use "Gittite" as an identification for a citizen of any but the Philistine Gath. Jonah was from Gath-hepher (2 Kgs. 14:25), but he is not described as a "Gittite"; rather, the text describes him as "the prophet, who was of Gath-hepher." If Obed-edom were from Gath-rimmon, he would not be identified as a "Gittite" but as a "man from Gath-rimmon." The invariable usage of the Old Testament thus proves that Obed-edom was a Philistine from the town of Gath. After a brief time in David's possession, the ark was back in Gentile hands.

That a Philistine was living in the environs of Jerusalem is no surprise. Philistines had occupied many towns of Israel before the

days of Samuel (1 Sam. 7:14) and they returned after the death of
Saul (1 Sam. 31:7). Moreover, David had close connections to the
city of Gath. He resided in Ziklag, a Gittite city, as a vassal of
Achish, king of Gath, during the last year and a quarter of Saul's
reign (1 Sam. 27:1–7), and when he returned to Israel a contingent
of Gittites accompanied him, similar to the mixed multitude that
came with Israel from Egypt. Together with the Cherethites and
Pelethites, the Gittites in his bodyguard numbered six hundred
fighting men (2 Sam. 15:18), and if we added their families the
number would be in the thousands. Obed-edom was perhaps in this
Gittite company that emigrated to Israel when David became king.

Some of David's Gittite allies became Gentile God-fearers.
Achish of Gath loved and defended David as Yahweh's anointed,
recognized him as an "angel of God," and swore to David in the covenant name of Yahweh (1 Sam. 29:6–10). If anything, Ittai expressed his faith even more dramatically when he determined to
follow David into exile rather than serve the usurper Absalom. Like
Achish, he swore in Yahweh's name that he would never abandon
David: "As Yahweh lives, and as my lord the king lives, surely wherever my lord the king may be, whether for death or for life, there
also your servant will be" (2 Sam. 15:21). This was a profession of
faith, an impressive act of discipleship. Thus, the fact that Obed-
edom was a Philistine does not mean he was a pagan. On the contrary, he was a Philistine convert.

Structural considerations also indicate that Obed-edom was a
Gentile and a Philistine. As I showed in *A House for My Name*, the
passage about the transfer of the ark to Jerusalem in 2 Samuel 6 is
chiastically related to the account of the Philistine capture of the ark
in 1 Samuel 4–6.[5] In that outline, the Philistine exile of the ark in
1 Samuel 5–6 matches the three-month sojourn of the ark in the
house of Obed-edom. While the ark was in Philistia, Yahweh bad-
gered the Philistines with plagues, but, in contrast, when the ark

[5] *A House for My Name* (Moscow: Canon, 2000), 140–149.

went to the house of Obed-edom, also a Philistine, it brought bless-ings. Thus, the structural arrangement of the passage suggests that there was a brief Philistine "exile" in 2 Samuel 6, as there was a longer one in 1 Samuel 4–6.

To reiterate, Gentile involvement with the ark was unprec-edented. Never during Israel's wilderness wanderings nor during the period of the judges did anyone outside the tribe of Levi guard and care for Yahweh's throne. Something new was going on. Around the time that David was preparing an undivided tent, Gentiles began to join the company of ark-ministers. To be sure, an event of "glo-bal" and "cosmic" significance was in the offing. An "eschaton" was on the horizon.

## Obed-edom the Levite

Nor did Gentile involvement end when the ark came to rest in Zion. Apparently, the story of Obed-edom continues. An "Obed-edom" appears among the ministers of the ark several times in 1 Chronicles 15–16. In the first reference, the name is included in a list of Levitical ministers and Obed-edom is identified as a "gatekeeper" for the ark (1 Chr. 15:18, 24). Verse 21 of the same chapter includes the name again, but instead of being a gatekeeper for the ark, this Obed-edom is a musician. Once the ark was placed in David's tent, "Obed-edom and Jeiel" were among those ap-pointed "as ministers before the ark of Yahweh, even to celebrate and thank and praise Yahweh God of Israel" (16:4; cf. 16:38). Finally, the name is found in 1 Chronicles 26 in a list of the Levites whom David appointed to serve as overseers of the temple storehouse (vv. 4–5, 8, 15; cf. 2 Chr. 25:24). Though it is possible that these pas-sages refer to different men named "Obed-edom," all the passages include Obed-edom among the Levites. To make the following dis-cussion clearer I will assume that they are all references to the same man and will call him "Obed-edom the Levite."

Chronicles also refers to Obed-edom the Gittite (1 Chr. 13:13–14; 15:25), and the question arises: Was Obed-edom the Gittite the same man as Obed-edom the Levite? It seems not. One, after all, is a Gittite and the other a Levite. If my argument that Obed-edom the Gittite was a Philistine was at all convincing, it seems to eliminate the possibility that Obed-edom might also be an Israelite and a Levite. Case closed.

Nonetheless, the possibility that the "Gittite" and the "Levite" were the same man is worth exploring, for several reasons. Contextually, by the time a reader comes to Obed-edom the Levite in 1 Chronicles 15:18, he has already been introduced to Obed-edom the Gittite, and the fact that the name appears without more precise identification at least leaves the possibility of confusion. The danger of confusion is even more evident in 15:24–25: Verse 24 names "Obed-edom and Jehiah" as gatekeepers and the following verse mentions the "house of Obed-edom." Verse 25 must be Obed-edom the Gittite, and the close juxtaposition of the names is either confusing, or perhaps a tantalizing hint that they are one and the same.

It would, moreover, be exceedingly odd if the ark were taken from Obed-edom's house without his participation. For three months, he had cared for the ark, guarded and kept it, and Yahweh had blessed his labors. Then one day David showed up, thanked Obed-edom for his efforts, and took the ark away, leaving Obed-edom standing in the doorway waving goodbye. It would seem natural for David to invite Obed-edom to move to Jerusalem to continue the work he had been doing. Why send a pink slip to a successful ark-guardian, especially when Israel had lately been singularly clumsy in her handling of the ark?

Looking at the wider context in Chronicles, it is striking that no Obed-edoms are listed in the Levitical genealogies, even among the "gatekeepers" (1 Chr. 9:17–27). Of course, thousands of Levites were unnamed in the genealogies, but those unmentioned in the genealogies are normally unmentioned everywhere else too. There is a striking disjunction between Obed-edom the Levite's comparative prominence in 1 Chronicles and his utter absence from the

genealogies. Other Levites who have plum offices at David's tent
or the temple *are* included in the genealogies. Asaph is linked with
Obed-edom the Levite as a minister before the ark in Zion (1 Chr.
16:37), and he appears in the Levitical genealogy (6:39). Of course,
Asaph was a very prominent Levite in David's time, the chief musician of the Levitical choir and orchestra, but Obed-edom, with his
sixty-eight "brothers" was also a prominent Levitical minister—
though he has no genealogy. The obscure "son of Jeduthun" is also
included among the Levitical ministers at the ark in Zion (16:38),
and his genealogy is provided (9:16). Meshelemiah is listed with
Obed-edom as a gatekeeper for the temple (1 Chr. 26:1–2, 9), and
he and his son Zechariah are listed in the genealogy of Levi (9:21),
though he is not mentioned anywhere else. Why would Obed-
edom, who is mentioned much more often in these chapters, lack
a genealogy? Is it perhaps because Obed-edom was not of Levitical
descent? Is it perhaps because Obed-edom the Levite was a Gittite?

Finally, the references to Obed-edom the Levite in 1 Chronicles
26 are oddly phrased in several respects. The chapter begins by trac-
ing the ancestry of Meshelemiah to Levi's son Korah (v. 1), and then
lists Meshelemiah's sons (vv. 2–3). Verse 4 introduces Obed-edom,
but (like Melchizedek) without genealogy. If he was a son of Korah,
why not mention it? Further, eight of Obed-edom's sons are listed
(vv. 4–5), and the Chronicler comments that "God had indeed
(Heb. *ki*) blessed him" (v. 5). Translating *ki* as "indeed" suggests that
the list of Obed-edom's sons *confirms* a point the Chronicler has already mentioned. Were I to say, "Indeed he is a fine violinist," you
would assume that I had previously been talking about his musical talent. If, on the other hand, I say, "The price of grain is wretch-
edly low," pause, and then add, "Indeed he is a fine violinist," you
will assume either that you missed some portion of the conversa-
tion or that I am mad. The large family of Obed-edom the Levite
confirms the Chronicler's previous claim that Yahweh had blessed
Obed-edom, but the only other reference to God's blessing an
Obed-edom is a reference to Obed-edom the Gittite: "Yahweh
blessed the family of Obed-edom with all that he had" (13:14).

To be sure, *ki* might be translated as a conjunction, in which case the clause would read "for God had blessed him." On this reading, the *ki*-clause of verse 5b might be taken as a conclusion to the initial clause of verse 4. Hence, "And Obed-edom had sons (parenthetical list) for God had blessed him." Even if this is the preferred translation, the Chronicler's reference to God's blessing on Obed-edom the Levite gatekeeper echoes with his earlier report about Yahweh's blessing on Obed-edom the Gittite caretaker of the ark. If the two Obed-edoms are different men, they are certainly beginning to look like twins.

Though these arguments do not amount to an irrefutable demonstration that Obed-edom the Gittite was the same man as Obed-edom the Levite, they are sufficiently strong to challenge any facile assumption that they were different men. Robert Gordon's conclusion that Obed-edom was rewarded with "Levitical preferment" for his service to Yahweh's throne is at least plausible,[6] and I believe that the weight of the evidence supports this conclusion.

### Provoked to Jealousy

So, let us assume that Obed-edom, a Philistine from Gath, was in fact incorporated into the Levitical company that served at the ark-shrine of David, and was later included among the gatekeepers of the temple. On what basis could this be justified? Given the fact that the Levites were a genealogically qualified priesthood (see Heb. 7), how could someone without a drop Levi's blood serve among Levites?

There are two possible answers to that question, one particular to Obed-edom, the other a more general point about the position

---

[6] *I & II Samuel: A Commentary*, Library of Biblical Interpretation (Grand Rapids: Zondervan, 1986), 233. P. Kyle McCarter (*2 Samuel,* Anchor Bible [Garden City: Doubleday, 1984], 170) attributes the Levitical genealogies to "later tradition," which "perhaps troubled by the consignment of the ark to the care of a foreigner, ascribed to Obed-edom a Levitical genealogy and remembered him as a musician . . . and gatekeeper." This is implausible, for had the Chronicler wished to elide Obed-edom's Gentile origins, why identify him as a "Gittite" in the first place (1 Chr. 13:13)?

of Gentiles in the Old Testament period. We take the general point first: throughout the Old Testament, it was common for people without blood ties to Abraham, Isaac, and Jacob to be incorporated into Israel. When Yahweh instituted the covenant of circumcision, Abraham had only one descendant but many servants (see Gen. 14:14). All of these servants and their sons were circumcised (Gen. 17:23), and thus became part of "Abraham's seed." From the beginning, then, the community of the circumcised was larger than the community of blood descendants of Abraham. Over the centuries, other "Gentiles" were grafted into Israel. Seventy blood descendants of Jacob migrated to Egypt (Gen. 46:26–27; Exod. 1:1–5), but Jacob had many servants (Gen. 32:4–5, 7), and it is likely that several of his sons at least had equally large households. Yet, when Israel came from Egypt, the distinction between Jacob's blood descendants and the descendants of Jacob's servants had evaporated; the people that came from Egypt were simply the "twelve tribes." Likewise, when Israel left Egypt, a "mixed multitude" went with them (Exod. 12:38), yet when Israel entered the land Israel was again simply "twelve tribes." Evidently, during the sojourn in Egypt and during the forty years of wandering in the wilderness, those who were not blood-related to Jacob were incorporated into one or another of the tribes of Israel. This is explicitly noted in the case of Caleb, a Kenizzite (Num. 32:12; Josh. 14:6; 14:14), who was incorporated into the tribe of Judah (Num. 13:6).[7] If "Gentiles" could be incorporated into other tribes, there would seem to be no bar to Gentiles being incorporated into the tribe of Levi. With only 22,000 males from a month and older (Num. 3:39), Levi was a small tribe when Israel came from Egypt. Yet, Levi's family could hardly have produced so many over the course of four generations in Egypt (Exod. 6:14–27). Many of the original Levites must have been from the "mixed multitude."

More specifically, Obed-edom received Levitical standing because he was so evidently approved by God for ministry before the

[7] James B. Jordan has frequently made this point in his writings and lectures.

ark. David must have jumped at the chance to include such a man among the ark's permanent ministers. I imagine him saying to the Levites, as Peter would say to the apostles many centuries later concerning Cornelius, "How can we refuse to include Obed-edom in the ministry of the ark, a man who has received the blessing of Yahweh in the same way that we have done?" Yahweh's blessings on Obed-edom demonstrated that he had been elected to serve.

*Tremble, All the Earth*

Of course, one Gittite does not constitute a trend. Is there other evidence that Gentile participation in Israel's worship increased in David's day? The psalm recorded in 1 Chronicles 16:8–36 certainly points in this direction. This psalm was the first sung before the ark on Zion (in fact, so far as we know, it was the first thing *ever* sung before the ark), and is typical of the psalms that were sung there. Several details of the psalm are important for our purposes.[8] First, as John Kleinig points out, the psalm is intended to "proclaim" Yahweh; it is a psalm "about" Him, and not merely a psalm directed "to" Him.[9] The initial exhortation of verse 8 urges Israel to "give thanks to Yahweh" and "call upon His name," but immediately adds the exhortation to "make known His deeds." Similar exhortations appear in verses 23 ("proclaim goods tidings of His salvation from day to day") and 24 ("Tell of His glory among the nations, His wonderful deeds among all the peoples"). Verse 31 reiterates the theme: "Let them say among the nations, 'Yahweh reigns.'"

---

[8] More extended discussions may be found in John Kleinig, *The Lord's Song: The Basis, Function and Significance of Choral Music in Chronicles* (*JSOT* Supplement #156; Sheffield: *JSOT* Press, 1993), 133–148; Tamara C. Eskenazi, "A Literary Approach to Chronicles' Ark Narrative in 1 Chronicles 13–16," in Astrid B. Beck, et. al., eds., *Fortunate the Eyes that See: Essays in Honor of David N. Freedman* (Grand Rapids: Eerdmans, 1995), 268–271; and Kirsten Nielsen, "Whose Song of Praise? Reflections on the Purpose of the Ps. in 1 Chronicles 16," in M. Patrick Graham and Steven L. McKenzie, eds., *The Chronicler as Author: Studies in Text and Texture* (*JSOT* Supplement #263; Sheffield: *JSOT* Press, 1999), 327–336.

[9] Several times Kleinig cites an article by P. A. H. de Boer that argued that the *le* in 1 Chronicles 16:9 and elsewhere should be translated as "about" rather than as "to." Hence, verse 9a reads: "Sing about Him, sing praises about Him." See Kleinig, *The Lord's Song*, 139, note 1.

As several of the quotations in the previous paragraph indicate, the exhortation to publicize, proclaim, and tell about Yahweh is addressed to the nations (vv. 23–24, 31). In fact, the psalm is structured as a series of concentric circles: initially, Israel is called to praise (vv. 9–22), then the nations join in (vv. 23–30), and finally the entire cosmos rejoices at Yahweh's coming and His enthronement in Jerusalem (vv. 31–33).[10] Not only Israel, but "the earth" is to proclaim the salvation of Yahweh (v. 23) and to recount His "wonderful deeds" (v. 24). As the nations join in Israel's song of praise, they are simultaneously encouraged to reject their idols, which are nothing (vv. 25–26). In context, verse 29 is especially striking: The series of exhortations to "ascribe" glory to the Lord is addressed to the "families of the peoples" (v. 28a), and this same audience is being addressed by the closing exhortation of verse 29: "Bring a tribute (*minchah*),[11] and come before Him; worship Yahweh in the glory of holiness." Thus, the "families of the nations" are being invited to join the worship of Israel.

Kleinig's summary of the progression of the psalm is apt:

> As they announced the Lord's sovereign presence and called on the congregation to remember the Lord by praising him, the singers also invited the Israelites to worship him as he had ordained. They urged the Israelites to seek the Lord's presence and strength regularly (16:11). They also invited the peoples of the world to relinquish their reverence for their deities and to recognize the sovereignty of the Lord by offering sacrifices to him and prostrating themselves as suppliants before him (16:28–29). In their praise the singers then invited Israel and all nations to receive strength and joy from the Lord in their common worship of him, which would lead to the proclamation of him and his goodness in their common praise.[12]

Like a pebble dropped into a pool, the song of Israel reverberates until it causes the seas to roar, the trees to sing, and the heavens to

---

[10] I am following Kleinig's outline here (Ibid., 143–144). Note again Eskenazi's comments about the "global" and "cosmic" dimensions of the praise described in the psalm ("A Literary Approach," 269–270).

[11] The word here is normally translated as "grain offering," but the word means tribute.

[12] Kleinig, *The Lord's Song*, 147.

ring with praise. Just as the Levitical singers were at the center of the
Chronicler's genealogies, so they sing now at the center of a universal
choir.

We are so used to Psalms and prophets inviting Gentiles to worship Yahweh that we forget how innovative it was in the time of
David. In the songs and hymns recorded earlier in Scripture, Gentiles are included only as enemies to be crushed, killed, dashed,
drowned, and hammered in the head. The Song of Moses and
Miriam is the earliest recorded psalm of Israel (Exod. 15:1–18). Israel celebrates because Pharaoh and his armies have been thrown
down into the sea (15:1, 4), covered in the depths like a stone (v.
5). When the other nations hear, "they tremble" and "anguish has
gripped the inhabitants of Philistia" (v. 14). Edom, Moab, and the
peoples of Canaan will melt before the Lord's burning anger (v. 15),
and, in general, "terror and dread fall upon them" (v. 16). Though
some Canaanites did convert when they heard about the exodus
(Josh. 2:8–13), the song does not contain the slightest hint of this.
At the exodus, the Gentile response to Yahweh was expected to be
terror, not trust.

Similarly, the song of Deborah (Judg. 5:1–31) acclaims Yahweh's
victory over the Canaanites. Deborah celebrates Israel's gathering for
battle, the Lord's triumph over the "kings of Canaan," and especially
Jael's clever assassination of Sisera, but the nations are not encouraged to participate in the celebration. The only passing allusion to
other nations comes at the end of the song: "Thus let all Thine enemies perish, O Yahweh" (v. 31). Hannah's song at the birth of
Samuel praises the Lord for the impending downfall of the wicked,
which, in context, includes the wicked Philistines who were then
ruling Israel. As in the song of Deborah, Hannah's song ends with
a reminder that "those who contend with Yahweh will be shattered"
since He "will judge the ends of the earth" (1 Sam. 2:10).

The book of Psalms includes similar songs of destruction and
judgment; there are enough iron rods and terrorized nations to
satisfy any great-souled warrior. But it is also rich in psalms that

encourage the Gentiles to turn to Yahweh, to rejoice in Him, to sing and be glad because Yahweh is King and Judge (e.g., Ps. 18:49; 22:27; 47:1; 57:9; 67:3–5; 117:1). Of course, Israel was always to be an instrument for bringing the nations to worship and serve Yahweh, but Israel's stance toward the nations shifted from one period of her history to another. Under the Davidic covenant, the nations were particularly encouraged to join in Israel's homage to God. They were encouraged to sing along.

Obed-edom's incorporation into the ministry of Levites is the most explicit example, but the psalm in 1 Chronicles 16 suggests that he represented other Gentiles who would also be incorporated into the worship of Israel, even if they were not given Levitical duties. Obed-edom thus provides an historical precedent for the hope that Gentiles would one day participate more fully in the worship of Israel. This comes to clearest expression in Isaiah 66:18–21:

> "For I know their works and their thoughts; the time is coming to gather all nations and tongues. And they shall come and see My glory. And I will set a sign among them and will send survivors from them to the nations: Tarshish, Put, Lud, Meshech, Rosh, Tubal, and Javan, to the distant coastlands that have neither heard My fame nor seen My glory. And they will declare My glory among the nations. Then they shall bring all your brethren from all the nations as a grain offering to Yahweh, on horses, in chariots, in litters, on mules, and on camels, to My holy mountain Jerusalem," says Yahweh, "just as the sons of Israel bring their grain offering in a clean vessel to the house of Yahweh. I will also take some of them for priests and for Levites," says Yahweh.

And in Isaiah 56:6–7:

> Also the foreigners who join themselves to Yahweh, to minister to Him, and to love the name of Yahweh, to be His servants, every one who keeps from profaning the Sabbath, and holds fast My covenant; even those I will bring to My holy mountain, and make them joyful in My house of prayer. Their burnt offerings and their sacrifices will be acceptable on My altar; for My house will be called a house of prayer for all the peoples.

Incorporation of Gentiles into the order of Levitical priests was to be a central feature of the "new heavens and new earth" that Yahweh promised to create (66:22). This was central to Israel's eschatology. We have seen that this is no ethereal, unachievable promise; it is not an airy nothing. Chronicles gives this hope a local habitation and a name. And that name is Obed-edom.

# 4
# Sacrifices of Praise

Solomon's temple was called a "house of prayer for all the nations," but even before Solomon built the temple David had established a "tent of worship for all nations" at Zion. The temple was a universal house of prayer precisely because it incorporated the worship of the Davidic tent, because Yahweh's throne was carried up to Solomon's temple, because "Zion" moved a bit north to Moriah. As the prophecies of Isaiah 56 and 66, quoted at the end of the last chapter, show, the incorporation of Gentiles was a central feature of Israel's eschatological hope, but that hope was grounded in history, specifically in David's establishment of worship. David's system of worship was a preview of the eschatological worship in the renewed Jerusalem, and with the pitching of the tent the foundation of the temple was already laid. Solomon's job was only to act as a Joshua to David's Moses.

Zion's eschatological atmosphere helps to explain the form of worship that David introduced at the ark-shrine. At the Mosaic tabernacle, Israel's worship centered on animal offerings. Different offerings were presented—ascensions, purifications, trespasses, communion sacrifices, and tributes of grain[1]—yet the ritual of worship was in some respects invariable. Apart from the tribute, which was offered in conjunction with animal offerings,

[1] For a brief defense of this terminology, see my *A House for My Name: A Survey of the Old Testament* (Moscow: Canon, 2000), 87–95.

all involved slaughter and dismemberment of an animal, presentation of its blood, and burning of at least a portion of its organs and flesh. As noted briefly in chapter 1, so far as we can tell from the information in the Pentateuch, this ritual was performed in silence.

This last statement requires some qualification. According to Leviticus 16:21, on the Day of Atonement the High Priest had to confess "all the iniquities of the sons of Israel, and all their transgressions in regard to all their sins" over the scapegoat. It seems likely that the worshiper confessed his sins over his individual offerings; the trespass, for example, required restitution (Lev. 5:14–6:7), and it would be odd if no acknowledgment of sin was included in the rite itself. Yet, the Law does not explicitly demand a verbal confession. Music, moreover, is mentioned only once. Trumpets were blown over ascensions and communion sacrifices at appointed times (Num. 10:10), including the Sabbath and new moon as well as certain annual feasts (Lev. 23:2–3).[2] Outside these passages, there is no explicit reference in the Levitical Law to words or music in worship.

Throughout the reign of David, the comparatively silent Mosaic worship continued to be performed before the Mosaic tabernacle in Gibeon. Offerings were made "continually morning and evening, even according to all that is written in the law of Yahweh, which he commanded Israel" (1 Chr. 16:39–40). Even at Gibeon, however, notable changes were introduced. In addition to the priests, David appointed Levites there "to give thanks to Yahweh, because His lovingkindness is everlasting," and this thanksgiving in song was accompanied by "trumpets and cymbals" and other "instruments for the songs of God" (1 Chr. 16:41–42). This combination of animal offerings and musical worship continued after the temple was built. In preparation for Solomon's temple, David organized a group of Levitical singers and musicians (1 Chr. 25:1–31), and there are ref-

---

[2] The first "appointed time' (*mo'ed*) listed in Leviticus 23 is the Sabbath. Assuming that the word is used in the same sense in Numbers 10:10, the trumpets would be blown over the Sabbath offerings, which were more abundant than the daily offerings (Num. 28:9–10). Perhaps the "first of your months" or "new moon festivals" are explicitly mentioned in Numbers 10:10 because they are not among the *mo'edim* listed in Leviticus 23.

erences to temple music throughout Chronicles (2 Chr. 5:11–14; 7:6; 23:13; 29:25–28; 34:12).

At the tent of David, music dominated worship even more thoroughly. The ark's ascension to Zion was reminiscent of Yahweh's descent to Sinai. At Sinai, the Lord's glory appeared with thunder and lightning, and the people heard "a very loud trumpet sound," which "grew louder and louder" (Exod. 19:16, 19). At Zion, the trumpet did not come from the glory-cloud, but from the people; Israel herself, and particularly the Levites, had become a human glory, resounding with the joyful noise of the angelic host. Led by priests blowing trumpets, Levitical musicians surrounded the ark with a cloud of sound as it was brought from the house of Obed-edom (1 Chr. 15:25–28). When the ark had been set in its tent, David assigned Asaph to head the Levites who were "to minister before the ark continually, as every day's work required" (1 Chr. 16:37), and the context makes it clear that this "ministry" was in song and instrumental music:

> [David] appointed some of the Levites as ministers before the ark of Yahweh, even to celebrate and to thank and praise Yahweh God of Israel: Asaph the chief and second to him Zechariah, then Jeiel, Shemiramoth, Jehiel, Mattithiah, Eliab, Benaiah, Obed-edom, and Jeiel, with musical instruments, harps, lyres; also Asaph played loud-sounding cymbals, and Benaiah and Jahaziel the priests blew trumpets continually before the ark of the covenant of God. (1 Chr. 16:4–6)

On some occasions, animals offerings were made at the Davidic tabernacle. The procession of the ark into Jerusalem was accompanied by "ascensions and communion sacrifices before God" (1 Chr. 16:1), and later Solomon offered animals before the ark (1 Kgs. 3:15).[3] Apart from these occasions, however, worship at the Davidic tent normally did not include bloody offerings. This is evident from 1 Chronicles 16:37–43, which draws a distinction between the

---

[3] Two points of interest may be noted here. First, Deuteronomy 12 seems to require that all sacrifices be offered at a central location, yet during David's time there were at least two places of sacrifice—Zion and Gibeon. Was this legitimate? The answer is *yes*, and the reason

Levitical ministry at the ark (in song) and the priestly ministry at Gibeon (with animal offerings). Distinct types of worship were being performed at the two locations. Worship at Zion overlapped with worship at Gibeon, since at both locations worship included both song and animal offerings; but Zion worship emphasized music, while at Gibeon the worship was mainly through ascensions and communion sacrifices.

The purpose of this chapter is to examine worship at the Davidic tabernacle, though at a few points passages dealing with a later period of Israel's history will be brought into play. My interest is not in the actual performance of music—instrumentation, performance customs, the style of music played—but in how the musical performance was understood. What metaphors and descriptions did the Chronicler use to make sense of this worship? Two main issues are discussed. First, by what right did David expand the musical component of Israel's worship? Was this a violation of the law? Was he given additional revelation? How is this change in Israel's worship consistent with the Law's insistence that worship had to be according to the "ordinance of Yahweh"? Second, I will show that song was understood, among other things, as a new form of sacrifice, the "sacrifice of praise." Chapter 6 deals more fully with music in temple worship, expands the discussion of the analogies between sacrifice and song, and thereby teases out some aspects of a theology of liturgical song.

In several passages, the Bible tells us that David received a plan for the temple and its worship from Yahweh. David told Solomon that "Yahweh made me to understand in writing by His hand upon me, all the details of this pattern" (1 Chr. 28:19), and the "pattern" included a plan for "the divisions of the priests and the Levites and for

---

is that worship was not centralized because the sanctuary was not fully established. Second, it is interesting to note that no purifications (sin offerings) were offered at the dedication of the Davidic tent. Apparently purifications could not be offered so long as the sanctuary and its worship was divided into two locations, since to offer a purification, you needed both the ark and the altar. In all likelihood, purifications were not offered at the sanctuary at Gibeon; without the ark, the purification system, including the Day of Atonement, could not function.

all the work of the service of the house of Yahweh" (28:13). In his description of Hezekiah's celebration of the Passover, the Chronicler reiterates the divine authorization of Levitical music:

> [Hezekiah] stationed the Levites in the house of Yahweh with cymbals, with harps, and with lyres, according to the command of David and of Gad the king's seer, and of Nathan the prophet; for the command was from Yahweh through His prophets. (2 Chr. 29:25)

David's liturgical innovations were, therefore, based on revelation. According to John W. Kleinig, however, there is more to the story. There are a number of hints in Chronicles that David's reorganization of worship was an application and expansion of Mosaic regulations. Kleinig discusses three main passages, two of which are discussed below. To Kleinig's insights I have added other considerations, often expanding points that Kleinig treats more briefly.

### Duties of Ministers under the New Moses

Most prominently, David cites or alludes to the Law when assigning duties to the priests and Levites. He quotes, for example, from Deuteronomy in his reminder that the Levites were responsible for carrying the ark. The regulation in Deuteronomy reads:

> At that time Yahweh set apart the tribe of Levi to *carry the ark* of the covenant of Yahweh, to stand before Yahweh to *serve* Him and to bless in His name until this day. (10:8)

And David instructed the Levites with these words:

> No one is to *carry the ark* of God but the Levites; for Yahweh chose[4] them to *carry the ark* of God and to *minister* to Him forever. (1 Chr. 15:2)

The word translated as "serve" in Deuteronomy 10:8 is *sharut*, and this is the same Hebrew word translated as "minister" in 1 Chronicles 15:2.

---

[4] As Kleinig points out, the reference to Yahweh's choice of Levi refers to Deuteronomy 18:5 (*The Lord's Song: The Basis, Function and Significance of Choral Music in Chronicles* [*JSOT* Supplement #156; Sheffield: *JSOT* Press, 1993], 34).

Though David virtually restated the Law's requirements, an examination of the structure of the passage reveals that the work he required of the Levites was quite different from the work required under the Mosaic system. Chapters 15–16 form a single unit, and this passage is divided into two large sections: 15:1–16:3 describes the procession of the ark into Jerusalem, while 16:4–43 explains David's arrangements for worship at Jerusalem and Gibeon. Both sections end with David's benediction, first placed on the people (16:2) and then on his household (16:43). The first section is itself divided in two. 1 Chronicles 15:15 refers to the commands of Yahweh through Moses, and thus forms an *inclusio* with David's citation of the Law in 15:2. Between these two references to the Law, the text describes the preparations for the transfer of the ark. Verses 15:16–16:3 then tell us that the Levites carried out this duty of transport. Overall, 15:1–16:43 may be outlined as follows:

A. Transport of the ark, 15:1–16:3
　　1. Organization for the procession, 15:1–15
　　2. The actual procession, 15:16–16:3
B. Ministry of the Levites and priests in Jerusalem and Gibeon, 16:4–43[5]

It is clear that the two main sections of this passage correspond to the two duties of Levites prescribed by Deuteronomy 10:8 and reiterated by David. 15:3–16:3 is concerned with the Levitical responsibility for transporting the ark, and the duty of "ministry" or "service" is detailed in 16:4–43. The verb *sharat*, which first appears at 15:2, is used again in 16:4 and 37, indicating that 16:4–43 gives details about the "ministry" that David mentioned in general terms

---

[5] For several reasons, I disagree with the analysis of this passage provided by Kleinig (ibid., 45). Kleinig argues that the duty of transport is covered in 15:4–15, and that the musical ministry is covered in 15:16–25. This fails, first, because 15:1–16:43 is a single unit of text, marked by a contrasting *inclusio*: Israel gathers in 15:3, and is not dispersed until 16:43. Second, the transport of the ark is not actually carried out until 15:25–16:3, so it is artificial to end the section on "bearing the ark" at 15:15. Finally, David uses the word *sharat* in 15:2, and the word does not appear again until 16:4; thus, 16:4 marks the beginning of the Chronicler's description of Levitical "ministry." Up to that verse, the Levites are engaged in "portage" and "service," but not "ministry."

in 15:2. The chart below summarizes the parallels:

| *Deuteronomy 10:8* | *1 Chronicles 15:2* | *1 Chronicles 15:3–16:43* |
|---|---|---|
| Carry the ark | Carry the ark | Levitical transport, 15:3–16:3 |
| Minister | Minister | Levitical ministry, 16:4–43 |

The important point here is that the "ministry" described in 16:4–43 is almost entirely ministry in song and instrumental music. Levitical singers and musicians are listed (16:4–6), a sample of Levitical song is inserted (16:7–36), and then David determines the personnel and form of worship that will continue during his reign (16:37–43). Yet, not a word about Levitical ministry of music is found in Deuteronomy 10:8 or elsewhere in the Pentateuch. Under the Mosaic system, Levitical "ministry" consisted of guarding the sanctuary, aiding priests in altar work, and assisting the people in their worship. Levites did not, however, sing or play musical instruments. Yet, David cites the Law as the basis for organizing the Levites as a musical troupe. *Sharat* or "service" has been transformed or expanded to encompass musical performance.

A related example of David's liturgical hermeneutics may also be explored. The verb for "carry" in 15:2 is the Hebrew *nasa'*, which is used to describe the Levitical transport of the ark in Numbers 4:15. Given the structural analysis offered above, 15:16–24 is within the subsection of this passage that has to do with the Levitical "bearing" of the ark; it is part of the passage covered by the verb *nasa'*. But 15:16–24 does not describe preparations for physical transport but organization for musical accompaniment. Thus, just as "ministry" (*sharat*) opened up to include musical ministry in 16:4–43, so also the duty of bearing the ark (*nasa'*) consists of lifting up the Lord in praise, as well as physical portage of His throne.[6]

A similar transformation is evident in two other verses of 1 Chronicles 15. Both speak of the role of Chenaniah in the procession

[6] Possibly, a pun is intended. The infinitive form of *nasa'* in 1 Chronicles 15:2 is *le-she't*, and the word *she't* means exaltation, dignity, nobility (see Gen. 4:7; 49:3; Job 13:11; 31:32; Ps. 62:5). Physically "bearing" the ark is being compared to "exalting" the dignity and glory of the One enthroned on the ark.

of the ark, and both use the word *massa'*, a noun form of *nasa'* used frequently in Numbers to describe the "burden" of the tabernacle furniture that the Levites were to carry (see Num. 4:19, 24, 27, 32, 47, 49). The translations below are from the New American Standard Bible (NASB):

> And Chenaniah, chief of the Levites, was in charge of the singing (Heb. *massa'*); he gave instruction in singing (Heb. *massa'*) because he was skillful. (15:22)

> Now David was clothed with a robe of fine linen with all the Levites who were carrying the ark, and the singers and Chenaniah the leader of the singing (Heb. *massa'*) with the singers. David also wore an ephod of linen. (15:27)

By the NASB translation, the verb normally used for the "load" of tabernacle furniture means "singing" in this passage.

This translation is, however, disputed. Walter Kaiser argues that

> The translation of *sar hammassa'* as the "leader of the music" is indefensible. The root meaning is "to lift," *not* "to utter." . . . the context deals with bearing the ark and *massa'* is the normal word in that context.[7]

Kleinig agrees that the word is best translated as "transportation" in 1 Chronicles 15:22, but offers the additional comment that the ambiguity about the meaning of *massa'* arises because Chenaniah was "in charge of the ceremonial procession for the occasion," which included both the ark's physical transport and musical accompaniment. He concludes that Chenaniah was "responsible for both the physical and musical 'transportation' of the ark."[8] Kleinig thus is open to the possibility that *massa'* is used somewhat metaphorically here.

A stronger case can be made for this conclusion. Verse 22 can be smoothly translated as "Chenaniah was chief of the Levites in transport; he gave instruction in transport for he had insight." Thus far,

---

[7] In R. Laird Harris, et. al., eds., *Theological Wordbook of the Old Testament*, 2 vols. (Chicago: Moody, 1980), 2:601.

[8] *The Lord's Song*, 47, n. 1.

Kaiser's point stands. But in verse 27, Kaiser's insistence that *massa'* does not have any musical connotations is more difficult to sustain. The verse is chiastically structured:

A. Now *David* was clothed with a robe of fine *linen*
  B. with all the Levites who were **carrying** [*nasa'*] the ark and the **singers**
  B'. and Chenaniah the leader of the *massa'* the **singers**
A'. *David* also wore an ephod of *linen*.[9]

As indicated by the bold type, B and B' share a reference to the "bearing" of the ark and to "singers," but "singers" in B' stands in an odd grammatical relation to the rest of the clause (as my translation has sought to indicate). It is not preceded by a preposition or a conjunction. Perhaps something has dropped from the text that would make the relation of the singers to Chenaniah clearer, but as it stands, one possible translation of verse 27 is, "and Chenaniah the leader of the transport *of* the singers."[10] If correct, this translation may imply only that the singers are part of the procession transporting the ark; but it seems to imply more, namely, that the singers are *doing* the transporting. Song, as well as shoulders, "bear up" and "lift up" the ark-throne of Yahweh, so that He rides into Zion "enthroned on the praises of Israel" (Ps. 22:3). The "burden" of the Levites is no longer merely a physical one but a musical one.

An examination of the Chronicler's use of *'abad* ("serve") and the related noun *'abodah* ("service") supports this conclusion. 1 Chronicles 6:31–32 (Heb. vv. 16–17) offers the first description of the Levitical choir:

Now these are those whom David appointed over the service of song in the house of Yahweh, after the ark rested. And they were ministering [*sharat*] before the tent of meeting, until Solomon built the house of Yahweh in Jerusalem. And they stood according to their ritual ordinance after their service [*'abodah*].

---

[9] This translation is my own.
[10] I wish to thank Peter Enns of Westminster Theological Seminary in Philadelphia for confirming the possibility that this is a "construct" or "genitive" construction.

Here, clearly, *'abodah* means musical performance. The same is true in David's instructions to the Levites as he organized them for ministry at the future temple of Solomon:

> David said, "Yahweh God of Israel has given rest to His people, and He dwells in Jerusalem forever. And also, the Levites will no longer need to carry [form of *nasa'*] the tabernacle and all its utensils for its service." For by the last words of David the sons of Levi were numbered, from twenty years old and upward. For their office is at the hand of the sons of Aaron with the service of the house of Yahweh, in the courts and in the chambers and in the purifying of all holy things, even the work of service [*'abodah*] of the house of God, and with the showbread, and the fine flour for a tribute, and unleavened wafers, or what is baked in the pan, or what is well-mixed, and all measures of volume and size. And they are to stand every morning to thank and to praise Yahweh, and likewise at evening, and to offer all ascensions to Yahweh, on the Sabbaths, the new moons and the fixed festivals in the number set by the ordinance concerning them, continually before Yahweh they are to keep charge of the tent of meeting, and charge of the holy place, and charge of the sons of Aaron their brothers, for the service of the house of Yahweh. (1 Chr. 23:25–32)

On the surface, the latter passage simply states that the Levitical duty of carrying the ark was canceled since the ark had come to a permanent home in the temple. A more careful reading, however, suggests that the duty was not canceled so much as transformed. *'Abodah* is commonly used in the Pentateuch to describe the Levites' duty of carrying the ark and other furniture of the temple; it means service or labor, but the specific form of labor involved was physical lifting and carrying (Num. 4:24, 27, 31, 49).[11] Though David said that the Levites no longer had the duty of *massa'*, they continued to have the duty of *'abodah*. But the two words in the Pentateuch refer to the same activity, the physical labor of transporting the tabernacle and its furnishings. Further, in this passage, the continuing duty of *'abodah* includes standing morning and evening to thank and praise Yahweh (v. 30). Physical labor, again, has become musical

---

[11] For details, see Jacob Milgrom, *Studies in Levitical Terminology I: The Encroacher and the Levites; The Term* 'Aboda (Berkeley: University of California Press, 1970), 60–87.

performance, and David has applied the Law's requirement that Levites perform 'abodah as a requirement that they sing.

Several passages from later portions of Chronicles indicate a similar shift in the meaning 'abodah. When Josiah called Israel to celebrate the Passover, he instructed the Levites,

> Put the holy ark in the house which Solomon the son of David king of Israel built; it will be a burden [massa] on your shoulders no longer. Now serve ['abad] Yahweh your God and His people Israel. (35:3)

As with David's instructions in 1 Chronicles 23, this seems to be a simple cancellation of the duty of carrying the ark, but when understood against the background of the Mosaic law, the passage is making a different point. Levites were to continue 'abodah, and the "service" that they performed included singing and praise (35:15). Further, 2 Chronicles 29:35b summarized the worship in the days of Hezekiah by saying that the king established "the service ['abodah] of the house of Yahweh." In context, this service consisted of offering ascensions, peace offerings, and libations (v. 35a), but in this passage animal sacrifices are explicitly coordinated with musical offerings (vv. 25–30). Thus, the re-established 'abodah of Yahweh's house includes the 'abodah of instrumental and choral music.

After the establishment of a permanent, fixed "place" for the Lord's throne and His house, the earlier Levitical duty of physically "transporting" and "servicing" the tabernacle and its furnishings was transformed into a musical "bearing" of God's name and throne. David applied and expanded the Levitical law, and in so doing radically revised the job description of the Levites, but he did this without canceling the Mosaic laws of worship. If the Levites were responsible for the physical "exaltation" of Yahweh's throne, they were also legitimately responsible for the verbal and musical exaltation of His name.

*Standing to Serve*

In other ways too, the Chronicler shows that David's reorganization of the Levites was rooted in Mosaic requirements. Typically, priestly ministry was summarized in the Law by the phrase "standing to serve."[12] Priests were given a literal and metaphorical "standing" in Israel's worship; they literally stood in places where no one else was permitted to stand, they had a position in Israel that no one else had, and they had this "standing" for the purpose of "serving." The priests were allowed to stand at the altar so that they could offer the "bread of God," permitted to enter the Holy Place to offer incense before Yahweh, and the High Priest was permitted to "stand" in the Most Holy Place to engage in a ministry of atonement for Israel. A priest was one who "stood" in order to "serve" (see Num. 16:9; Deut 10:8; 17:12; 18:5; 1 Kgs. 8:11; 2 Chr. 5:14; 29:11; Ezek. 44:11, 15).

In 1 Chronicles, this language is adapted to describe the musical ministry of priests and Levites. We have already seen how the verb "serve" (*sharat*) is applied to musical ministry, and the same is true of the verb "stand" (*'amad*). According to 1 Chronicles 15:16, "David spoke to the chiefs of the Levites to appoint their brothers the singers, with instruments of music, harps, lyres, loud-sounding cymbals, to raise sounds of joy." "Appoint" here translates a form of *'amad* and means "cause to stand." Thus, David "caused the Levites to stand" before the ark to "minister" in music. In obedience to David's instructions, the Levites "caused to stand" Heman the son of Joel, and others (15:17). The two verbs come together in 1 Chronicles 6:31–33a:

> Now these are those whom David appointed [*'amad*] over the service of song in the house of Yahweh, after the ark rested there. And they ministered [*sharat*] with song before the tabernacle of the tent of meeting, until

---

[12] See the discussion in Kleinig, *The Lord's Song*, 39–40; my article, "Attendants of Yahweh's House: Priesthood in the Old Testament," *Journal for the Study of the Old Testament* 85 (1999): 15–20; and, more comprehensively, my *The Priesthood of the Plebs: The Baptismal Transformation of Antique Order* (Eugene, Ore.: Wipf & Stock, forthcoming).

Solomon had built the house of Yahweh in Jerusalem; and they stood ['*amad*] according to their office over their order. And these are those who stood ['*amad*] with their sons . . .

Mosaic terminology (stand and serve) is thus used to describe the ministry of song, even though the Law never mentions Levites "standing" for a "ministry" of song. A "standing" or "position" originally established for slaughtering animals and caring for the Lord's house becomes a "standing" for the purpose of praise.[13]

Levitical singers, moreover, were organized into *mishmeret* or "watches" (1 Chr. 25:8; NASB translates the word as "duty").[14] The Hebrew noun comes from the verb *shamar*, which means "to guard," and the noun and verb are used together in several passages in Numbers to refer to the guard duty of priests and Levites at the Mosaic tabernacle (1:53; 3:7; 8:26; 18:3–5).[15] At the tabernacle, the Levites literally guarded the doorways and were armed to prevent unauthorized Israelites from intruding on holy space. When 1 Chronicles 25:8 uses the noun in a context that describes the duties of Levites in the temple, Israelites familiar with the Law would doubtless recall the passages concerning guarding the house. Just as the Levites once "did guard duty" at the tabernacle, now they are divided into groups of "guardians" at the temple. Yet the form of guard duty has been transformed or at least has received an additional dimension; instead of (or, perhaps, in addition to) killing intruders, the Levitical guards now "do guard duty" by singing and playing musical instruments. Musical performance is described under the metaphor of guard-duty.

The tools and implements of priestly and Levitical ministry were also expanded to include musical instruments.[16] The Hebrew word

---

[13] 1 Chronicles 16:4 is a related passage, but uses slightly different terminology. The word translated as "appoint" in the NASB is *natan*, "give," but the word "ministers" is a noun form of *sharat*.

[14] Kleinig, *The Lord's Song*, 41–42.

[15] Milgrom, *Studies in Levitical Terminology*, vol. 1, esp. 8–16.

[16] Kleinig, *The Lord's Song*, 77–78. Kleinig seeks to distinguish between "holy vessels" that were used by priests in the sacrificial ritual and "vessels of service" used by Levites in

used for musical "instrument" (*keli*; e.g., 1 Chr. 15:16; 16:5) was
also used for "utensils" employed in the ministry of the altar—forks,
basins, pitchers, bowls, snuffers, etc. These are called "utensils (*keli*)
of service in the house of Yahweh" and "utensils (*keli*) for every kind
of service" (1 Chr. 28:13–14).[17] In David's time, musical "utensils"
were an additional category of "instruments for the service of
Yahweh."

The parallel of sacrificial "utensils" and musical "instruments" is
also suggested by the fact that both were classified according to degrees of value and holiness. I noted in the previous chapter that the
materials and furniture of the Mosaic tabernacle were organized by
a graded system of value, from the bronze altar in the court, to the
wood-and-gold furniture of the Holy Place, to the pure gold of the
ark-cover and cherubim. Similarly, there were utensils of bronze (2
Chr. 4:16), silver, and gold (1 Chr. 28:14, 17). With regard to musical instruments, the gradation did not correspond to the materials used but to the persons who performed with the instruments.
Priests blew trumpets (1 Chr. 15:24; 16:6, 42), Levites ministered
with cymbals, harps, lyres, and voices (1 Chr. 15:16, 28; 16:5; 25:1,
3, 6), while the people of Israel seem to have participated in worship mainly with their voices (1 Chr. 16:36b). As can be seen from
the chart below, the gradation of musical instruments replicates the
gradation of persons and space:

---

"secondary aspects of the ritual" (78). Though different phrases are used for the temple vessels,
and some such distinction is implied in 1 Chronicles 9:28–29, the phrases are not always
used in the way that Kleinig's claims. He cites 2 Chronicles 5:5 to illustrate the use of "holy
vessel" (78, n. 1), but that passage refers to the instruments used by Levites in the service
before the ark, not to sacrificial vessels used by the priests; by Kleinig's definitions, they should
be called "instruments of service." On the other hand, he cites 1 Chronicles 23:26 to support
his interpretation of the phrase "vessels of service" (78, n. 2), but this verse speaks of the
Levitical duty of carrying the "vessels" of tabernacle service, and this would include the holiest
objects in the Mosaic system. Thus, the two phrases can be used interchangeably.

[17] The word "service" here translates *'abodah*, the normal word for Levitical transport or
portage of the tabernacle furniture.

| Status of Person | Space | Instrument |
|---|---|---|
| Priest | Holy Place | Trumpet |
| Levite | Courtyard (assisting priest) | Harp, Lyre, Cymbal, etc. |
| Israelite | Courtyard | Voice[18] |

Again, we see David applying the Mosaic ceremonial law in fresh ways. The classification of sacrificial "utensils" has been applied to musical "utensils."

## Levitical Clans

One final indication that the Davidic system of worship was an application of the law has to do with the distribution of duties among the clans within the Levitical tribe.[19] Levi had three sons, Kohath, Merari, and Gershon, and, according to Numbers 4, each group was given responsibility for transporting a particular portion of the Mosaic tabernacle. The particular assignments are shown in the chart below:

| Clan | Work |
|---|---|
| Kohath | Furniture, Num. 4:1–20 |
| Gershon | Curtains, 4:21–28 |
| Merari | Frame, pillars, sockets, 4:29–33 |

When David established the musical form of Levitical *'abodah* at his tent in Jerusalem, the three Levitical clans were again assigned

[18] For descriptions of these various instruments, see, in addition to articles in standard Bible dictionaries and encyclopedias, Kleinig, *The Lord's Song*, 77–89; J. H. Eaton, "Music's Place in Worship: A Contribution from the Psalms," in *Prophets, Worship and Theodicy: Studies in Prophetism, Biblical Theology and Rhetorical Analysis and on the Place of Music in Worship* (Leiden: Brill, 1984), 85–107; Philip J. King, "The Musical Tradition of Ancient Israel," in Prescott H. Williams, Jr. and Theodore Hiebert, eds., *Realia Dei: Essays in Archaeological and Biblical Interpretation in Honor of Edward F. Campbell, Jr.* (Atlanta: Scholar's Press, 1999), 84–99; Ulrich S. Leupold, "Worship Music in Ancient Israel: Its Meaning and Purpose," *Canadian Journal of Theology* 15 (1969), 176–186; Othmar Keel, *The Symbolism of the Biblical World: Ancient Near Eastern Iconography and the Book of Psalms* (trans. Timothy J. Hallett; New York: Crossroad, 1985), 335–352.

[19] Kleinig provides much of the material for the following discussion but does not present this specific line of argument. But see James B. Jordan, "1 Chronicles and Levites" (Lecture Outline for Eleventh Annual Biblical Horizons Summer Conference, 2001), 14.

specific duties. According to 1 Chronicles 6:33–47, Heman was the central singer (v. 33), with Asaph at his right hand (v. 39) and Ethan at his left (v. 44). And these three chief musicians were from different clans of the Levites: Heman was a Kohathite, Asaph a Gershonite, and Ethan from the clan of Merari (vv. 33, 39, 44). Though the duties of Levitical ministry had changed, the Mosaic clan structure remained in place.

Intriguingly, David's appointments did not follow what might be the expected distribution of duties. Heman, the Kohathite, along with Ethan (called Jeduthun), was assigned to Gibeon to minister with the priests at the tabernacle of Moses (1 Chr. 16:41–42), while Asaph, the Gershonite, was left with his brothers to minister before the ark (16:37). From the Law, one would have expected Kohathites to minister before the ark. To be sure, there is a logic to David's arrangement, insofar as the Kohathite Heman ministered in the place where most of the tabernacle furniture was located. Yet, the association of the Gershonites with the ark was new, and was perhaps related to the transfer of priestly privilege from the house of Eli to the house of Zadok. Since there is a change in law and covenant, there is a corresponding change in priesthood and in the distribution of responsibility among the Levites who serve with the priests. In this instance also, we see David enforcing the Mosaic liturgical law (by dividing up the Levites by clan) but also adjusting it to new circumstances (by reassigning responsibilities).

### Memorial Song

David's assignments to the Levites and priests grew out of an application of the law, and the musical worship they performed was also understood according to Mosaic categories. Here, as Kleinig points out, the chief Mosaic source was Numbers 10:9–10.[20] According to 1 Chronicles 16:4, David "appointed some of the Levites as ministers before the ark of the Lord, even to celebrate and to thank and praise the Lord God of Israel." The allusion to Numbers

---

[20] *The Lord's Song*, 34–37.

10 is found in the verb "celebrate," which translates *hazkir*, a form of the verb *zakar*. Normally, *zakar* means "remember," as in the name "Zechariah," which means "Yah remembers." In fact, nowhere else does the NASB translate this verb as "celebrate." Specifically, the verb form of *zakar* used in 1 Chronicles 16:4 means "to cause to remember," and the Authorized Version is closer to the Hebrew here: David "appointed certain of the Levites to minister before the ark of the Lord, and to *record* and to thank and praise the Lord God of Israel." Thus, the Levitical ministry of music was designed not only to please and glorify Yahweh by thanks and praise, but also to "cause Him to remember."

Musical performance is also described as a memorial in the Law. According to Numbers 10, Yahweh instructed Moses to make two silver trumpets, which would be used for mustering the troops for battle and at certain points in Israel's worship:

> And when you go to war in your land against the adversary who attacks you, then you shall sound an alarm on the trumpets, that you may be remembered (a form of *zakar*) before Yahweh your God, and be saved from your enemies. Also in the day of your gladness and in your appointed times, and on the first of your months, you shall blow the trumpets over your ascensions, and over the communion sacrifices of your peace offerings; and they shall be a memorial (*zikaron*) of you before your God. I am Yahweh your God. (Num. 10:9–10)

As indicated in the parentheses, the Hebrew verb translated "may be remembered" is a passive form of *zakar*, and behind the noun "reminder" or "memorial" in verse 10 is the Hebrew *zikaron*, formed from the same verb. Thus, the one explicit reference to worship music in the Pentateuch employs the notion of "memorial," and this was the basis for David's instructions to the Levites concerning their choral worship.

## Music and Sacrifice Under David [21]

The analogy underlying all these transformations of terminology and practice is that between musical performance and animal

[21] Ibid., chap. 4.

sacrifice. In addition to the passages discussed above, Chronicles makes it clear that the Levitical choir and orchestra were offering a "sacrifice of praise." Music was understood under the metaphor of sacrifice.

Song at the Davidic tabernacle was coordinated with the offering of sacrifice at the Mosaic tabernacle in Gibeon, and these forms of worship were later combined into a single service in the temple. The coordination of the spatially separated worship during the days of David is evident from several of the terms used to describe the musical worship of the Levites. According to 1 Chronicles 16:37, Asaph and his brothers sang before the ark in Jerusalem "continually, as every day's work required," and both "continually" and "every day's work" are Levitical terms.[22] "Continually" translates *tamid*, a technical term for the morning and evening offerings at the Mosaic tabernacle. Exodus 29:41–42 prescribes an ascension offering of a lamb every evening and morning, as a "continual [*tamid*] ascension throughout your generations at the doorway of the tent of meeting before Yahweh." In Numbers 28–29, the same word is used some seventeen times, always with reference to the daily ascension offering. Numbers 28:3–4 requires "two male lambs one year old without defect as a continual [*tamid*] ascension every day. You shall offer the one lamb in the morning, and the other lamb you shall offer at twilight" as "a continual [*tamid*] ascension which was ordained in Mount Sinai as a soothing aroma" (28:6). On the appointed days of the calendar, additional animals were offered, but these were always above and beyond the *tamid* offerings. Two additional lambs served as "the ascension of every Sabbath in addition to the continual [*tamid*] ascension and its libation" (28:10; cf. 28:15, 24, 31; 29:6, 11, 16; etc.). When *tamid* is applied to the musical ministry at the tabernacle of David, the idea is not that the Levites sang around the clock, but that they sang while the *tamid* ascensions were being offered at Gibeon (see 1 Chr. 16:40).

---

[22] Ibid., 74–75.

The phrase "as every day's work required" or some similar phrase is used in connection with the appointed times or feasts of Israel.[23] Leviticus 23:37 summarizes the liturgical calendar of Israel with these words: "These are the appointed times of Yahweh which you shall proclaim as holy convocations, to present food offerings to Yahweh—ascensions and tributes, communion sacrifices and libations, *each day's matter on its own day.*" Again in 2 Chronicles 8:12–13, Solomon kept the appointed times prescribed by the Mosaic law "according to the daily rule," and the restoration community celebrated the Feast of Booths by offering the prescribed number of ascensions "as each day required" (Ezra 3:4). Thus, this phrase refers specifically to the additional animal offerings provided for Israel's feast days; to the *tamid* offerings were added offerings "according to the daily rule." Both terms are applied to musical performance, and this implies that songs were sung at Zion at the time of the daily offerings, and apparently a heightened musical performance took place on feast days, to coordinate with the heightened sacrificial worship.

In a number of passages, the temporal coordination of music and sacrifice is explicitly described. In 1 Chronicles 23:30–32, David instructs the Levites in their duties at the future temple:

> And they are to stand every morning to thank and to praise Yahweh, and likewise at evening, and to offer all ascensions to Yahweh, on the Sabbaths, the new moons and the fixed festivals in the number set by the ordinance concerning them, continually before Yahweh. Thus they are to do guard duty at the tent of meeting, and the guard duty of the holy place, and the guard duty of the sons of Aaron their brothers, for the service ['*abodah*] of the house of Yahweh.

Note especially here that the conclusion we reached by examining the use of *tamid* is perfectly explicit: Levites are to stand and sing "morning and evening." This passage also confirms that "thanks and praise" has been added to the "service" of the Levites: Given the usage in the Pentateuch, we expect the text to say that the Levites are "to stand every morning to serve," but instead we read that they "stand in order to thank and to praise." Song has become a form of "service"; the ascent of sound before Yahweh delights Him just as the ascending smoke soothes His anger. Other passages in Chronicles show that music and sacrifice were offered together in the temple, and these will be examined in chapter 6.

For the moment, we may conclude from the Chronicler's use of Levitical terminology that sacrificial ministry and sacrificial worship did not cease when the ark was placed in the tent on Zion. Though no blood was shed, no altar erected, no smoke ascended, yet sacrifice was still taking place. The ark had ascended to its place; it is the beginning of the end. At such a moment, nothing is more natural than song. At such a moment, the Levites begin to offer their bodies as living sacrifices, their voices ascending to Yahweh in a cloud of song.

# 5
# The Booth of David

As we have seen in the two previous chapters, the tabernacle of David and its worship was an important development of Israel's worship, but, as the scattered hints about eschatology have indicated, it is also important typologically. As noted in the introduction, David's tent was the one and only sanctuary that was built on Zion. "Zion," and certainly Zion terminology and symbolism, was transferred to the temple mount when Solomon took the ark up to Moriah and set it in the temple, but the original source of the hope of Zion was the tabernacle of David. I have also pointed out that the prophets always expressed the hope of Israel in terms of a restored Zion, never in terms of a restored Moriah. Thus, the institutions that David established on Zion loom very large in the eschatological program of ancient Israel. One passage in particular, Amos 9:11–12, makes an explicit connection with the tabernacle of David, and this passage is all the more significant because of the role it played in the deliberations of the early church at the council of Jerusalem (Acts 15:12–21). These passages will be the focus of attention in this chapter, but it must be recalled that Amos 9 is one among many passages that might be treated.

The discussion will proceed in several stages. After looking at Amos 9 to set some context for verses 11–12, I argue that the historical referent of the phrase "booth of David" is the ark-tent established on Zion. Consideration of the larger context in Amos will confirm that identification and will show that Amos specifically promised the revival of the choral worship of David's tent. Turning to the New Testament, I examine the use of Amos's prophecy at the Jerusalem council, and finally sketch the broader typological picture.

## Return from Exile

According to Amos 9, the restoration of the Davidic booth would occur as the endpoint of a series of events that will repeat the events of David's initial rise to power. As we noted earlier, the ark was exiled in Philistia after the battle of Aphek, and David brought it to Jerusalem only after it had spent many decades in the house of the Gentile Abinadab in the Gentile city of Kiriath-jearim. Similarly, Amos 9 begins with Yahweh's threat to abandon His people and send them into exile. Yahweh gives the command to "smite the capitals so that the thresholds will shake, and break the heads of them all" (9:1), which has to do with the destruction of the nobles and leaders of Israel, pictured as pillars. Like Eli and his sons before the battle of Aphek, the pillars of Israelite society have become Satanic, and so their heads/capitals will be broken (cf. Gen. 3:15). As for the remainder of Israel, those who are simple stones in the house will also suffer the judgment of exile. There will be no escape, as verses 3–4 emphasize in a chiastically structured warning:

A. No escape in Sheol, v. 2a
  B. No escape in heaven, v. 2b
  B'. No escape on the summit of Carmel, v. 3a
A'. No escape on the floor of the sea, v. 3b

Whether they seek escape from Yahweh by digging down or by climbing up, He will search them out. Even exile, the climactic curse of the covenant (Deut 28:64–68), will provide no protection: "though they go into captivity before their enemies, from there I will command the sword that it slay them, and I will set my eyes against them for evil and not for good" (v. 4). Though Yahweh threatens to "shake the house of Israel among all nations as grain is shaken in a sieve" (v. 9), He also promises to "restore the captivity of My people Israel, and they will rebuild their ruined cities and live in them" (v. 14); He will "plant them on their land, and they will not again be rooted out from their land which I have given them" (v. 15).

As the Lord sends Israel into exile, he turns his back on them and treats them as just another idolatrous nation. Israel's special status is radically relativized: "'Are you not as the sons of Ethiopia to Me, O sons of Israel?' declares Yahweh" (v. 7). If Israel protests that the exodus distinguished them from the nations, and proved their special standing in the world, Yahweh has a response (v. 7): "Have I not brought up Israel from the land of Egypt, and the Philistines from Caphtor and the Arameans from Kir?" Israel's exodus was not so unique after all; Philistines and Arameans likewise have their exodus traditions. Yet, Yahweh promises that he will not utterly destroy Israel. Though they are shaken among the nations like grain from a sieve, "not a kernel will fall to the ground" (v. 9), and though they have been driven from the land, "days are coming" in which their prosperity will be renewed, and they will be forever re-planted in the land (vv. 13–15)—an Edenic land where the mountains drip wine and the hills dissolve. In this context comes the promise that David's booth would be restored, its walls and breaches repaired, and Israel exalted above Edom and other Gentile nations.

Thus, Amos 9 predicts this sequence of events: exile, Yahweh turns to the Gentiles, Israel restored, and Israel exalted. This recapitulates the history of the ark before and during David's reign. Thus, Amos 9 leads us to expect that the restoration will be described in Davidic terms.

*Raising Up the Fallen Booth*[1]

And so it is. Amos describes the restoration of Israel after exile in these terms:

> "In that day I will raise up the fallen booth of David, and wall up their breaches; I will also raise up his ruins, and rebuild it as in the days of old;[2] that they may possess the remnant of Edom and all the nations who are called by My name," declares Yahweh who does this.

Verse 11 is structured as follows:

In that *day*
> I will *raise up* the booth of David which has fallen
> > and wall up their breaches
> > and his ruins I will *raise up*
> > > and rebuild it
> as in the *days* of old.

Thus, the *inclusio* of "day" and "days" indicates that the coming day of restoration will recapitulate days of old, and specifically of the days of David. As everywhere in the prophets, Amos taught that the restoration of Israel would be a return to the halcyon days of David.

The word "booth" itself refers to a makeshift and temporary shelter, and in most of its uses refers to the "booths" constructed

---

[1] I have dealt with this passage in a more rigorous form in an unpublished article, "The Booth of David, Amos 9:11–12."

[2] In translating the pronouns, I have followed W. C. Kaiser, "The Davidic Promise and the Inclusion of the Gentiles (Amos 9:9–15 and Acts 15:13–18): A Test Passage for Theological Systems," *Journal of the Evangelical Theological Society* 20 (1977), 101–102. The first suffix is a feminine plural ("their breaches"), which Kaiser takes as an indication that Amos has in view the future healing of the breach between Israel and Judah. The second suffix is masculine singular ("his ruins"), and Kaiser sees this in straightforward typological fashion as a reference to the resurrection of Christ; in context, "his" could only refer to "David." Only the final suffix (a feminine singular, agreeing with the feminine singular of "booth") refers to the booth ("rebuilt it"). Thus, the verse offers a complete redemptive history in pronominal form: reunion of Israel-Judah, the resurrection of Jesus, and the erection of the kingdom of God. Though I believe Kaiser is correct, the translation of the pronouns affects my treatment of this passage very little.

by Israel during the Feast of Booths (called "Succoth" or "booths").
Amos's promise that the restoration of Israel would involve the restoration of the fallen "booth of David" (*sukkat dawyd*) has been
interpreted in a variety of ways.[3] A number of scholars see the phrase
as a political image, but disagree about the specific referent. Some
interpret it as a promise of a restored Davidic dynasty,[4] while another asserts that the Davidic booth is "nowhere else mentioned"
and concludes it is an innovative "simile for the Davidic kingdom."[5]
For others, the booth represents the Davidic empire, and for that
reason Amos refers to Israel's dominance of Edom (v. 12). None of
these opinions is convincing. While there is clearly a political and
even international dimension to the prophecy (v. 12), the Davidic
dynasty is elsewhere called a house (*bayt*) rather than a booth (e.g.,
2 Sam. 7:11), and the word *sukkah*, which normally connotes a
flimsy, makeshift, or at least temporary structure, hardly serves as
an image of a restored kingdom or empire.

As an alternative, H. Neil Richardson proposes that *sukkat* (read
as *sukkot*) names a place, rather than an object, hence Yahweh's
promises to "restore David's fallen Succoth." Richardson's argument
relies in part on the conclusion that 2 Samuel 11:11 and 1 Kings
20:12 refer not to military "tents" but to the Transjordanian city of
Succoth. According to Richardson, Succoth served as a base of operations for David's incursions to the east, and securing Succoth
made it possible for David to control Rabbah of the Ammonites, especially as "one of the most important roads linking both Jerusalem
and Shechem to Syria passes through Succoth." As a result, "Succoth
became a city associated with David's victories and development of

---

[3] H. Neil Richardson reviews the various options in "SKT (Amos 9:11): 'Booth' or
'Succoth'?" *Journal of Biblical Literature* 92 (1973), 375–376.

[4] Kaiser, "The Davidic Promise and the Inclusion of the Gentiles," 101; Richardson,
"SKT," 475 cites Harper and Cripps, while Dupont quotes from Haenchen to this effect ("'Je
rebâtirai la cabane de David qui est tombeé' (Ac 15, 16 ' Am 9, 11)" in E. Gräßer and O.
Merk, *Glaube und Eschatologie: Festschrift für Werner George Kümmel* [Tübingen: Mohr,
1985], 22).

[5] M. D. Terblanche, "'Rosen und Lavendel nach Blut und Eisen': Intertextuality in the
book of Amos," *Old Testament Studies* 10/2 (1997), 315.

his empire."[6] Richardson's conclusions, however, certainly go beyond his evidence. Were Succoth as crucial to David's strategy as he suggests, it is odd that it is, even on his own accounting, mentioned only once in the historical accounts of David's wars. Further, the one reference that Richardson discovers, 2 Samuel 11:11, is not convincing. 2 Samuel 11:1 states explicitly that Joab had gone out to besiege Rabbah of the Ammonites, yet on Richardson's interpretation, verse 11 places Joab in "Succoth," some twenty-five miles northwest of Rabbah. Conducting a siege from such a distance would be cumbersome to say the least, especially since David controlled Transjordanian cities and territory much closer to Rabbah (see, e.g., the census route taken by Joab in 2 Samuel 24:5–7).

Ådna, by contrast, takes *sukkat* as a reference to the Jerusalem temple, which in Amos's day had fallen into disrepair. Citing several texts from the Psalms, he argues that the Bible itself refers to the temple as a *sukkah*, and he finds further support in Akkadian, Mesopotamian, and Egyptian parallels.[7] Though Ådna's emphasis on the sanctuary brings out an important nuance of Amos 9:11, his claims are finally not persuasive. As I argue below, the psalms he mentions do not refer to the temple of Solomon, and *sukkah* would, in any case, be an odd description of a permanent building (but cf. 1 Chr. 23:32). More decisively, though David planned and organized the work of the temple, he did not build it, and the temple is (understandably) never described as "David's temple," much less "David's booth."

Several pools of argument coagulate in the conclusion that Amos is referring to the tent that David pitched on Mount Zion: the usage of the word "booth," the context of Amos 9, and the larger context of Amos's prophecy. These will be discussed in turn.

    [6] "SKT," 377–379.
    [7] J. Ådna, "Die Heilige Schrift als Zeuge der Heidenmission: Die Rezeption von Amos 9, 11–12 in Apg 15, 16–18," in Ådna, et. al., eds., *Evangelium, Schriftauslegung, Kirche: Festschrift für Peter Stuhlmacher* (Göttingen: Vanderhoek and Ruprech, 1997), 14.

*Yahweh's Shelter*

To begin, several passages use *sukkah* to describe David's ark-shrine on Zion. In 2 Samuel 11:11, the word "booths" is used to describe the military encampment of Israel, but Uriah states that "the ark" also was "dwelling in a *sukkah*." Possibly Uriah was saying that the ark was on the battlefield with Israel and Judah, but he does not include the ark among those who are "camping in the open field," and this suggests that he was distinguishing the location of the ark from the location of the army. Within the larger context of 2 Samuel, it has already been stated that the ark was placed in a tent (2 Sam. 6:17) and that it was dwelling "in tent curtains" (*btwk hyry'h*, 2 Sam. 7:2), and two details connect 11:11 with these earlier passages. First, in both 11:11 and 7:2 the ark is said to "dwell" (*yashab*), and nowhere else in the narratives of David is this word used in connection with the ark. Second, thematically, Uriah's refusal to take ease while the ark was "dwelling in a booth" is reminiscent of David's earlier recognition of the incongruity of his living in a "house of cedar" while the ark "dwells within tent curtains" (2 Sam. 7:1). In 2 Samuel 11, David is seen lazing around in his cedar house while the ark was in a booth, in contrast to his zeal for the ark in chapter 7. David, once so concerned with the ark, is trumped by Uriah, who, though not even an Israelite, shows more respect for Yahweh's throne than does Yahweh's anointed. Given these parallels, the "booth" of 11:11 appears to refer to the "tent curtains" of 7:2.

Several psalms from the time of David provide more conclusive evidence that David's tent-shrine was known as a "booth."[8] One of these is Psalm 27, identified as a "Psalm of David." Verses 4–6 state:

[8] The texts discussed here are among those listed by Ådna, but he takes them as references to Solomon's temple. If the attribution to David at the beginning of the psalms is taken seriously, however, the psalms cannot refer to the temple, which was not built in David's time. My argument thus depends on my accepting psalm inscriptions as (at least) early and reliable tradition. For an argument that the titles are canonical, see D. Kidner, *Psalms* (Tyndale Old Testament Commentary; Downers Grove: InterVarsity, 1973–1976), 32–46. R. K. Harrison, also a conservative on this point, admits that some titles may be the work of a later

One thing I have asked from Yahweh, that I shall seek: That I may dwell in the house of Yahweh all the days of my life, to behold the beauty of Yahweh and to inquire in his temple. For in the day of trouble he will conceal me in his booth [*be-sukkah*]; in the secret place of his tent [*'ohel*] he will hide me; he will lift me up on a rock. And now my head will be lifted up above my enemies around me; and I will slaughter in his tent [*'ohel*] sacrifices with shouts of joy; I will sing, yes, I will sing praises to Yahweh.

This portion of the psalm focuses on the Lord's dwelling as a place of refuge and protection, and David refers to this dwelling as Yahweh's "house" and "temple" as well as his "booth" and "tent." The "tent" is, furthermore, clearly a place of worship, where David hopes to offer "sacrifices with shouts of joy" and to "sing praises to Yahweh." Structurally, "booth" is parallel to "tent" (v. 5):

He will conceal me
    in the booth
        in the day of evil
He will hide me
    in the secret place of his tent.

This suggests that *sukkah* and *'ohel* both refer to a sanctuary where David finds safety in the Lord's presence and worships him. In David's day, worship, as we have seen, was divided between the Mosaic tent in Gibeon and the ark-tent in Zion (1 Chr. 16:37–43), and Psalm 27's reference to a "booth" and "tent" must refer to one

editor (*Introduction to the Old Testament* [Grand Rapids: Eerdmans, 1969], 977–983). By contrast, some critics, such as Mowinckel and Childs, have argued that the titles are unreliable. On the specific psalms in question, one point stands strongly in favor of the originality or at least the earliness of the ascription. A later editor assigning a title to a psalm that includes a reference to the temple (such as Ps. 27:4) could be expected to assign the psalm to a poet who lived *after* the temple was built; to assign such a psalm to David would be recognizably anachronistic and would invite contradiction: "This cannot be a Davidic psalm because it mentions the temple." Assignment of a temple psalm to the time of David, thus, is evidence that the psalm did in fact come from the time of David, rather than from a later editor. My argument does not depend on any particular interpretation of *le* in the psalm titles; a psalm composed "to David" would be dated to the time of David as much as one composed "by David." For discussion, see P. C. Craigie, *Psalms 1–50* (Word Biblical Commentary #19; Waco: Word, 1983), 33–35.

of these. Though either is possible, the Zion tent is the more likely. Zion had become the central place of worship for Israel, since it was Yahweh's shrine in the capital city and since it was located in David's stronghold. Neither Samuel nor Chronicles, moreover, ever shows David worshiping at Gibeon.

Another Davidic psalm that refers to a "booth" is 31:19–21:

> How great is thy goodness, which thou hast stored up for those who fear thee, which thou hast wrought for those who take refuge in thee, before the sons of men! Thou dost hide them in the secret place of thy presence from the conspiracies of man; thou dost keep them secretly in a booth [*sukkah*] from the strife of tongues. Blessed be Yahweh, for he has made marvelous his lovingkindness to me in a besieged city.

Here, the "booth" is less a place of worship than simply a place of refuge from enemies. Yet, the structural arrangement of v. 20 is illuminating:

> Thou dost hide them
>   in the secret place of Your face
>     from the conspiracies of man
> Thou dost shelter them
>   in the booth
>     from the wrangling of tongues.

"Booth" is poetically parallel to the "secret place" where Yahweh's "face" or presence is known, and the booth is thus not merely a shelter but a shelter in the presence of Yahweh, a sanctuary of some sort. Literally, the referent would most likely be to the tent of the ark in Zion.

Both of these passages use the verb "hide" or "shelter" (*satar*) or the related noun (*seter*), and two other Davidic psalms speak of being "hidden" and "sheltered" in the shadow of Yahweh's "wings":

> Guard me as the apple of the eye; in the shadow of thy wings hide [*satar*] me.  (Ps. 17:8)

Let me sojourn in your tent forever; let me take refuge in the shelter [*satar*] of thy wings. (Ps. 61:4 [Heb. v. 5])

Though the image of seeking protection under the wings of Yahweh is complex, it at least pictures a worshiper finding shelter under the wings of the cherubim that form the Lord's ark-throne (cf. Exod. 25:17–22; 1 Sam. 4:4; 2 Sam. 6:2). The connection of the "wings" with the sanctuary is explicit in Psalm 61:4, for it is in the tent that David seeks protection under the wings of Yahweh. Here, the literal referent must be the ark-shrine of Zion, for David is seeking refuge under the wings of the cherubim on the ark. The use of *satar* in Psalms 27 and 31, therefore, plays into a complex of images that includes shelter in Yahweh's dwelling and under his wings. This strengthens the likelihood that the "booth" mentioned in these psalms is the Davidic ark-shrine.

Finally, the clearest use of "booth" as a description of the tabernacle of David comes from Psalm 76:1–3, a psalm of Asaph, a contemporary of David:

God is known in Judah; his name is great in Israel. And his booth [*sukkah*] is in Salem; his dwelling place also in Zion. There he broke the fiery shafts of the bow, the shield, and the sword, and the battle of war.

Note the parallelism in v. 2 (again following the Hebrew word order):

And it is in Salem
    his booth
and his dwelling place
    in Zion.

This psalm states explicitly what was ambiguous in the other psalms, namely, that the booth is located in "Salem" (Jerusalem) and specifically in "Zion." Further, the central parallelism indicates that the booth is a dwelling of Yahweh, a point strengthened by the fact that the Hebrew word for "dwelling place" (*ma'on*) was used for the tabernacle at Shiloh (1 Sam. 2:29, 32). Thus, the parallelism indicates that the booth on Zion was a sanctuary, a place where Yahweh was present. This must refer to the tent that David established for the ark in Jerusalem.

Returning to Amos 9:11, we conclude that the phrase *sukkat dawyd* has precedent in poetic descriptions of the ark-shrine in Zion, and this is the institution of David's time that would most naturally be described this way. Amos is thus promising the restoration of David's ark-shrine in Jerusalem.[9]

## The Noise of Israel's Songs

Examination of the overall structure of Amos's prophecy supports this conclusion. By analyzing this structure, we can grasp the specific force of the promise made to Israel in Amos 9:11–12. Amos's prophecy may be divided into two large sections.[10] Amos 1:1 says that the book contains the "words of Amos, who was

[9] The remaining clauses of Amos 9:11, however, present a difficulty for this interpretation. Though it makes sense to "raise up" (*qum*) a booth or tent, it seems to make little sense to speak of "walling up its breaches," "raising its ruins," or "rebuilding it as in days of old." These clauses seem to assume a permanent structure—a city or a house—that would not be easily described as a "booth." At a purely grammatical level, Kaiser's attention to the person and gender of the pronouns resolves this problem; the only verbs that are specifically used in conjunction with the "booth" are "raise up" and "build," both of which may, without difficulty, be applied to a "booth" (see Kaiser, "The Davidic Promise," 101–102, and the footnote above). More thematically, Amos seems to be indicating that the restoration will go beyond the central promise of a restored "booth" to encompass the "stronghold" of Zion, the city of David, and Jerusalem as a whole. During his reign, David not only established Zion as the central place of worship for Israel, but also repaired and built up the city (2 Sam. 5:9, 11). Further, as Ådna suggests, Isaiah 1:8 uses *sukkah* to describe the whole city of Jerusalem, and this could be an extended meaning in Amos as well. Thus, I would slightly modify his conclusion: Amos is referring not to the "unity of temple and city" but to the "unity of ark-shrine and city" ("Die Heilige Schrift als Zeuge der Heidenmission," 15). Further evidence for this approach is provided by the parallels between Amos 5:1–6:14 and 9:1–5, discussed below. Finally, 1 Chronicles 6:31 seems to refer to the ark-shrine on Zion as "the house of Yahweh," since the ark-shrine was the initial form of the temple. Thus, architectural imagery appropriate to the house was applied to the tent.

[10] I am building on the discussion in A. van der Wal, "The Structure of Amos," *Journal for the Study of the Old Testament* 26 (1983), 107–113. See now D. A. Dorsey, *The Literary Structure of the Old Testament: A Commentary on Genesis-Malachi* (Grand Rapids: Baker, 1999), 277–286, who sees the book as a heptamerous chiasm centering on 5:1–17.

among the sheepherders from Tekoa, which he saw in visions concerning Israel." This opening verse thus introduces two categories
of revelation—words and visions—and the book divides fairly
neatly into a book of words and a book of visions. Chapters 1–6
begin with Yahweh roaring from Zion (1:2), and these chapters
record the words of Yahweh in a third-person narrative. Beginning
in chapter 7, however, two striking stylistic changes take place:
Amos begins writing in first person (7:1 states that "Master Yahweh
showed *me*), and, instead of recording the words of Yahweh, Amos
begins recording scenes that Yahweh has *shown* him (the phrase
"Master Yahweh showed me" recurs in 7:1 and 7:4, and similar
phrases introduce 7:7, 8:1, and 9:1).

The beginning of the final section of chapters 1–6 is difficult to
locate. According to David Dorsey, 5:1–17 forms a single chiastic
outline, and the next section covers 5:18–6:14,[11] but there are several reasons to doubt this conclusion. First, after Yahweh's initial
"roar" from Zion, the "word" section is structured by the repeated
introductory exhortation, "Hear this word" (3:1; 4:1; 5:1; cf. also
8:4). If, as it seems, this phrase is used to introduce a new section
of the text, then the final portion of chapters 1–6 begins at 5:1
("Hear this word") and covers 5:1–6:14. Further, there are significant *inclusios* that link the early part of chapter 5 with the final section of chapter 6. 5:7 employs a vivid and unusual image by
condemning "those who turn justice into wormwood and cast righteousness down to the earth," and 6:12 reiterates the Lord's hostil-
ity to those who "turned justice into poison, and the fruit of
righteousness into wormwood."[12] Finally, 5:1–6:14 has a generally
chiastic internal arrangement, as the following outline shows (the
verbal connections between corresponding sections have been highlighted):

---

[11] Dorsey, *Literary Structure*, 281–282.
[12] Dorsey finds a questionable *inclusio* between "snake" (5:18) and "poison" (6:12), even
though there is no reference to poison in 5:18.

A. 5:1–7: "ten left," 5:3; "wormwood," 5:7; "righteousness," 5:7

   B. 5:8–15: "darkness," 5:8; *inclusio* on "hate," 5:10, 15; "vine
   yards," 5:11; "wine," 5:11

   B'. 5:16–6:8: "vineyard," 5:17; "darkness," 5:18; "hate," 5:21,
   6:8

A'. 6:8–14: "ten left," 6:9; "wormwood," 6:12; "righteousness,"
   6:12

Though it is possible that 5:1–6:14 might be further subdivided, it should be treated as a single unit of text.

The boundaries of the last of the "visions" section (i.e., chapters 7–9) are much easier to determine. Just as the "word" section of Amos is structured by exhortations to "hear," each subsection of the "vision" portion of the prophecy is introduced by the verb "see." 9:1 begins with "I saw," and the verb "saw" is the same in Hebrew as the word "showed" in 7:1, 4, 7, and 8:1 (*ra'ah*). 9:1–15 thus records the last of Amos's visions.

There are a remarkable number of parallels between the final "oracle" in 5:1–6:14 and the final "vision" in 9:1–15. Some of these are strictly parallel, in the sense that Amos says the same thing in both passages. More often, however, the later passage reverses the earlier, so that chapter 9 reverses the judgments of chapters 5–6. A number of these links are listed below.

1. Chapter 5 opens with a dirge over the house of Israel, imagined as a "fallen" virgin that will not rise up (vv. 1–2). Like the virgin Israel, the booth of David is also "fallen," and the same verb (*nafal*) is used in 5:2 and 9:11. Similarly, the verb "rise up" (*qum*) is used twice in 5:2, and appears again in 9:11 to describe the erection of the booth of David. Thus, 9:11 promises the raising of what had fallen in chapter 5.[13]

2. 5:8–9 introduces Yahweh as the one who

made the Pleiades and Orion and changes deep darkness into morning, who also darkens day into night, who calls for the waters of the sea and pours

[13] M. D. Terblanche, "'Rosen und Lavendel,'" 315.

them out on the surface of the earth. Yahweh is His name. It is He who flashes forth destruction upon the strong, so that destruction comes upon the fortress.

Though the substance is somewhat different, a structurally similar paean is found in 9:5–6:

> And Master Yahweh of hosts, the one who touches the land so that it melts, and all those who dwell in it mourn, and all of it rises up like the Nile and subsides like the Nile of Egypt; the One who builds His upper chambers in the heavens, and has founded his vaulted dome over the earth, He who calls for the waters of the sea and pours them out on the face of the earth. Yahweh is His name.

Both passages stress God's sovereign control of creation, and particularly of the sea, and both include the ringing affirmation that the God who does all this is named Yahweh.

3. In 5:11, Amos threatens that those who plant vineyards will not live to enjoy the wine, while 9:14 explicitly reverses this threat with the promise that "they will also plant vineyards and drink their wine."

4. 5:18–19 describes the "day of Yahweh" that will bring darkness and cause many to flee. There will be no escape; the one who escapes the lion will find himself confronted by a bear, and the one who gets away from the bear will be bitten by a snake. Likewise, 9:3 emphasizes that there is no escape from the wrath of Yahweh; neither those who dig into hell nor those who ascend to heaven will find safety (v. 2), for the Lord will "command the serpent and it will bite them" (v. 3). Both passages use the same word for "snake" (*nahash*) and the same (punning?) verb for "bite" (*nashak*). Neither the noun nor the verb is used elsewhere in Amos's prophecy.

5. 5:18 warns that those who long for the "day of Yahweh" will be disappointed, because the day will be darkness and not light, but 9:11 promises a restoration "in that day" and great prosperity in the "days" to come (9:13).[14]

---

[14] W. A. G. Nel makes a similar connection in "Amos 9:11–15—An Unconditional Prophecy of Salvation during the Period of the Exile," in J. A. Loader and J. H. le Roux, eds., *Old Testament Essays* (Pretoria: University of South Africa, 1984), vol. 2, 91.

6. According to 5:19, the lion, bear, and snake will attack the man who "flees" (*nus*), and the same verb is used twice in 9:1. Apart from these verses, Amos uses the verb only in 2:16.

7. 5:27 explicitly states the covenant curse of "exile [*galah*] beyond Damascus." Though the terminology is not the same, 9:4 also warns that Israel is destined to "go into captivity before their enemies."

8. Yahweh is called "God of hosts" in 5:27 and 6:14, and 9:5 calls Him "Yahweh of hosts." Between 6:14 and 9:5, Amos does not use "hosts" at all.

9. In 6:1–3, Yahweh compares Zion and Samaria to surrounding Gentile nations, and the comparison is not flattering to Israel. Similarly, in 9:7 the Lord calls Israel "sons of Ethiopia" and says that Philistines as well as Israelites can boast of an exodus.

10. Yahweh's hatred is directed specifically against the "city," Jerusalem, in 6:8, and the next reference to "cities" in Amos is found in 9:14, where Yahweh promises to "rebuild the ruined cities" of Israel, certainly including Jerusalem.

11. 5:26 uses the highly unusual word *sikkuth*, which differs in only one consonant from the word for "booth" in 9:11.

These parallels are sufficient to establish that the final "oracle" and the final "vision" correspond to one another, and several of these parallels indicate the overall relationship between the two passages: Like much of Amos, 5:1–6:14 is a relentless prophecy of judgment; but on point after point the Lord promises in 9:1–15 to reverse these judgments.

These overall parallels and reversals confirm that Amos was prophesying about the revival of the joyous worship of the Davidic tent in 9:11–12. One of the central points of 5:1–6:14 has to do with the corruption of Israel's worship, and the Lord's rejection of that worship. Amos records some of the most severe words of Yahweh found in Scripture:

> I hate, I reject your festivals, nor do I delight in your solemn assemblies. Even though you offer up to Me ascensions and your tributes, I will not accept; and I will not look at the peace offerings of your fatlings. . . . Master Yahweh has sworn by Himself, Yahweh God of hosts has declared: "I loathe the arrogance of Jacob, and I hate his citadels." (5:21–22; 6:8)

Yahweh not only rejects the animal offerings of Israel, but has grown tired of their music: "Take away from me the noise of your songs; I will not even listen to the sound of your harps" (5:23). He pronounces a woe against "those who are at ease in Zion" (6:1), who enjoy their sacrificial feasts of flesh and wine and who "improvise to the sound of the harp" (6:5–6) while ignoring justice, mercy, and the other weighty matters of the law. Because of this hypocrisy, Yahweh threatens to silence the songs of Zion.

Strikingly, the Lord compares these idle revelers to David who "design musical instruments for themselves" (6:5). The latter clause is often translated as "compose songs" (NASB), but the phrase is *keli-shir*, the very phrase used in Chronicles to describe "instruments of song." The first time Amos mentions David, he alludes to his role as a musician and as an organizer of worship music. Elsewhere, Amos mentions David only in 9:11, the passage concerning the booth of David. Given the inverse relationship between 5:1–6:14 and 9:1–15, the reader expects the second reference to David to promise a reversal of the first. That is the specific force of the "booth of David" prophecy: Israel's worship, Yahweh promised, would one day be restored.

Israel was populated in Amos's day by would-be Davidic musicians, who had David's aesthetic tastes but wholly lacked his passion for righteousness, but Amos's promise was that "on that day" a true royal song-leader would be given. In Amos's day, "woes" were pronounced against the worshipers of Zion, but "on that day" the booth of David would be restored. Though presently the Lord refused to listen to the song of Israel's harps, the promise that the tent of David would be restored is a promise that He would one day again take delight from Israel's praise. Silence, darkness, and gloom were about to descend on Israel, but Yahweh would one day turn mourning into dancing, and silence into new song.

## *With This The Prophets Agree*[15]

Amos's prophecy of a restored Davidic sanctuary and worship is quoted at a crucial juncture in the early church's main theological and practical struggle: the place of Gentiles in the New Covenant Israel. The issue centered on the question of whether or not Gentiles had to be circumcised to be incorporated into the people of God, the people of Abraham, Isaac, Jacob, and Jesus. The issue came to a head when Paul began to launch missionary efforts to Gentile territories from Antioch. A church had been established in Antioch by Christians fleeing the persecution that broke out after the martyrdom of Stephen. According to Luke's account, men from Cyprus and Cyrene "came to Antioch and began speaking to the Greeks also, preaching the Lord Jesus" (Acts 11:20). Barnabas and Saul were called to Antioch to help with the growing church (Acts 11:22–26), and the fact that the original audience for the gospel consisted of "Greeks" and that the disciples became known as "Christians" suggests that the church had a large proportion of Gentile believers, and thus provided a reasonable base of operations for Gentile missions.

After Paul's first missionary journey, he returned to Antioch and remained there some time (Acts 14:26–28). While he was there,

> Some men came down from Judea [i.e., to Antioch] and began teaching the brethren, "Unless you are circumcised according to the custom of Moses, you cannot be saved." And when Paul and Barnabas had great dissension and debate with them, the brethren determined that Paul and Barnabas and certain others of them should go up to Jerusalem to the apostles and elders concerning this issue. (Acts 15:1–2)

As a result, the apostles gathered in Jerusalem to consider the question of circumcision, and more broadly the question of the relation of Gentiles to the law of Moses.

[15] This and the following section especially represent more a "work in progress" than definite conclusions. More so than elsewhere, I feel that here I have not yet reached the peak.

Their final decision was that the church would not demand circumcision, but the council did require that Gentiles "abstain from things sacrificed to idols and from blood and from things strangled and from fornication" (15:29). Two lines of argument were presented as grounds for this conclusion. First was Peter's testimony concerning his experience with the household of Cornelius (Acts 10–11). When the Holy Spirit fell on the Gentiles at Cornelius's house, Peter concluded that "God, who knows the heart, bore witness to them, giving them the Holy Spirit, just as He also did to us," and this witness was a sign that "He made no distinction between us and them" (15:8–9). As he said at the time, "surely no one can refuse the water for these to be baptized who have received the Holy Spirit just as we did" (10:47). Since God had shown His approval of Gentiles, and since the house of Cornelius experienced a kind of Pentecost, no man could reject the Gentiles.

James, the chief elder of Jerusalem, offered the second line of argument. Reminding the council of Simon's testimony concerning the Lord's mercy to Gentiles, he went on to argue that Simon's experience fulfilled prophecy, and specifically the prophecy of Amos:

> And with this the words of the Prophets agree, just as it is written, "After these things I will return, and I will rebuild the tent of David which has fallen, and I will rebuild its ruins, and I will restore it, in order that the rest of man may seek the Lord, and all the Gentiles who are called by my name, says the Lord, who makes these things known from of old. (15:16–18)

James's quotation differs from the Hebrew original in several details. First, the clause "I will return" in verse 16 does not appear in the Hebrew at all. This clause is found in other prophecies of Israel's restoration from exile, and James may well be conflating the Amos prophecy with others.[16] The second difference between Amos

---

[16] In Jeremiah 12, the Lord says that He has forsaken His house and abandoned His inheritance (v. 7). As the passage progresses, it becomes clear that the house of Israel is the main referent; she is the "beloved of My soul" who has "roared against Me" and become "like a speckled bird of prey to Me" (vv. 8–9). Because of Israel's rebellion, and especially because of the desolation wrought by Israel's shepherds (vv. 10–11), the Lord threatens to "uproot

9 and James's quotation is that "Edom" in Amos 9:12 has become "mankind" or "man." Theologically, the change is perfectly legitimate, since Amos 9:12 promises that the nations who are called by the name of Yahweh will, with Edom, come under the dominion of Israel. Lexically, the change may represent a reading of the Hebrew that changed "Edom" to "Adam." Thus, the restoration of the Davidic tabernacle is understood as holding implications for all the sons of Adam. Third, instead of talking about Israel's possession of the nations, James speaks of the nations "seeking" the Lord (Acts 15:17). This has no basis in the text of Amos 9, but is perhaps an adjustment of language to the situation of the new covenant. Instead of Israel "possessing" nations in an imperialistic fashion, the new Israel's imperial conquest will occur as the nations seek the Lord.

None of these changes affect the substance of the Amos passage, and it can therefore be asked what James thought he was proving by quoting Amos. How is Amos 9:11–12 relevant to the question of Gentile inclusion and circumcision in particular? To understand this citation fully, we must recall two pieces of historical background. The first is the ark narrative in Samuel, which formed the background to Amos's prophecy. As discussed briefly above, these narratives cycle through a similar series of events three times. At the battle of Aphek, due to the sins of Eli and his sons, the ark was captured and taken into exile in Philistia. Though apparently defeated, Yahweh humiliated Dagon and caused plagues throughout the land, so that the Philistines were only too happy to send the ark out of their territory (1 Sam. 4–6). In the second sequence, the men of

---

them from the land" (v. 14). Yet, the threat is also to the temple-house, which represents the people-house and which was destined to be taken into exile as well (Jer. 52). Yet, "after I have uprooted them, I will again have compassion on them; and I will bring them back, each one to his inheritance and each one to his land" (12:15). The clause "I will again have compassion" may be translated as "I will return, and have compassion" (AV). This would be a fitting quotation to add to the Amos passage, since both are promising return from exile, a promise of compassion for fallen Israel. Yahweh promises to "return" also in Malachi 3:7. After the messenger comes with the announcement that Yahweh's purging fire is coming, the Lord offers reconciliation: "Return to Me, and I will return to you," said Yahweh of hosts.

Beth-shemesh sinned against the ark, and the ark left Israel again (out of Beth-shemesh, 1 Sam. 6:19–7:2). Sent to a Gentile city (Kiriath-jearim), it remained in a Gentile's house for a century (Abinadab). After a lengthy and apparently uneventful stay in Kiriath-jearim, the ark was restored to Israel (David's first attempt to bring it to Jerusalem, 2 Sam. 6:1–5), but Uzzah touched the ark and died (2 Sam. 6:6–11), and the ark was sent away from Jerusalem to the house of a Gentile (Obed-edom the Gittite). After three months it returned to Israel and ascended to Zion with great celebration (2 Sam. 6:12–19). The cycles are summarized in the chart below:

| Cycle | Sin | Ark with Gentiles | Effect | Return |
|---|---|---|---|---|
| 1 | Eli and sons | Philistia | Plagues | To Beth-shemesh |
| 2 | Men of Beth-shemesh | Kiriath-jearim (Abinadab) | Blessing | To Zion (failure) |
| 3 | Uzzah | House of Obed-edom | Blessing | To Zion (success) |

As soon as David had installed the ark in Zion, he conquered surrounding lands, including Edom (2 Sam. 8:1–14). With Yahweh enthroned in the midst of Israel, Israel began to spread out over the land.

As noted above, according to Amos 9, this same sequence would be repeated yet again "in that day": Israel would be cast away into exile (vv. 1–4); Yahweh would embrace Gentile nations as equal to Israel (vv. 7–10); but then Israel would be restored and conquer the surrounding nations (vv. 11–15). And, just as Gentiles were brought into Israel's worship at the booth of David, so Amos prophesied that Gentiles would "one day" be incorporated into Israel even more fully. Verse 12 promises that when the booth and the city have been restored, then Israel will come into possession of Edom. Reference to "Edom" in the context of a discussion of the "booth of David" is reminiscent of Obed-edom, who was instrumental in bringing the ark into Zion, into David's booth. Beyond Edom, Israel's dominion in its restored Davidic glory will extend to all the nations "who are called by My name." When the Lord turns from His anger and begins to delight again in the songs of Zion, Gentile voices will again be mingled with Israel's.[17]

Thus, the dynamics of the Jew-Gentile relation were very much a part of Amos's prophecy, and of the historical events underlying his prophecy. James discerned that Amos's prophecy was being fulfilled—not merely the few verses he cites but the whole sequence:

| David's time | Amos | Apostolic church |
|---|---|---|
| Ark in exile among Gentiles | Lord turns to Gentiles | Lord turns to Gentiles |
| Ark-shrine | Restored booth | Raising up of Jesus? |
| Obed-edom incorporated | Edom and nations | Gentiles added |
| Open access | Renewed open access | Open access; no circumcision |
| Israel restored | Israel restored | Israel restored |

Even if I am wrong that the Gittite Obed-edom was incorporated into the company of Levitical ministers, his story (and the story of Abinadab) represents an Old Testament preview of what Paul calls a "provocation to jealousy" (Rom. 11:11, 14). Salvation was offered to the Gentiles, Paul said, to make Israel jealous, and one of the goals of Paul's own ministry was to provoke such jealousy among his countrymen. When Jews saw that the God of Abraham had turned His attention to Gentiles, they would seek reconciliation, and "if their transgression be riches for the world and their failure be riches for the Gentiles, how much more will their fulfillment be!" (Rom. 11:12). The same dynamic was at work in David's time. When Israel saw that the Lord was pouring out blessings on Gentile caretakers of the ark, they were provoked to seek

---

[17] While the phrase *sukkat dawyd* focuses attention on the ark and its shrine, the political dimension of Amos's prophecy is clearly present. As discussed in chapter 3, the fact that David sat enthroned "before Yahweh" symbolized the exaltation of the Davidic house in Israel and among the nations. Though Amos's prophecy does not refer in the first instance to the restoration of the Davidic dynasty, kingdom, or empire, the symbol of "David's tent" is sufficiently rich to encompass that hope as well.

those blessings for themselves by bringing the ark into the midst of Israel. And the same dynamic was at work in the church's mission to the Gentiles. James's citation of Amos meant not only that Gentiles could join the worshiping throngs on Zion, but also that this inclusion of Gentiles would be a means toward the ultimate redemption of Israel. And the redemption of Israel would mean the redemption of the world.[18]

If James were only interested in finding scriptural support for the hope that Gentiles would one day be joined with Israel, any number of passages would have sufficed. Understood against the historical background of David's tent, Amos 9 fit the apostolic situation so much more precisely. He recognized that the Lord's turning to Gentiles would not only bless them, but was part of the promised restoration of Israel. He recognized that he and the other apostles had reached the "beginning of the end," and was looking for the salvation of all Israel.

## The Typology of David's Tabernacle

Against this background, we can now offer some tentative conclusions about the broader biblical-theological significance of David's tabernacle. Why did Yahweh establish His house in Jerusalem in this particular sequence? Why not simply move directly into a temple? Why was the ark-shrine the first sanctuary in Jerusalem?

---

[18] My main purpose is not to refute charismatic uses of Amos 9 and Acts 15, but I must make at least a few comments. A number of charismatics have taken Amos 9 to be a prophecy specifically about the charismatic renewal; the joyful and rambunctious worship of the charismatic churches is the restoration of David's tent. This runs clean contrary to James's interpretation of the prophecy, since he obviously saw the fulfillment of the prophecy occurring before his eyes. For some writers, moreover, the fulfillment of Amos 9 in the charismatic movement has provided grounds for abandoning noncharismatic churches. Graham Truscott, for example, urges his readers to "come out" from the dead and silent churches at Gibeon and join the Davidic worship on Zion (*The Power of His Presence: The Restoration of the Tabernacle of David* [Burbank, CA: World Map Press, 1969], 318–319). Not only does he fail to note that song was introduced into the worship at Gibeon (1 Chr. 16:39–42), but his characterization suggests that noncharismatic churches are hardly churches at all. Truscott wrote in the late 1960s, and I have no idea if the Davidic tabernacle is still used in this way today. If it is, it is an attack on the gospel, for it implies that something other than Christ unifies the church.

And how does the logic of this sequence shed light on the events of
the apostolic period? How is David's tent a type of the New Covenant?

We may begin by considering again the fulfillment of the prophecy of Amos 9. It has been suggested that Amos's prophecy can be
interpreted either in a "Christological" or "ecclesiological" manner.[19]
To suggest that these are alternative interpretations is nonsensical.
The church is the body of Christ, and therefore every type or prophecy of Christ is equally a prophecy about His church, what Augus-
tine called the *totus Christus*. And, of course, vice versa. Amos's
prophecy of a restored Davidic booth is both a promise fulfilled in
Jesus, and a promise fulfilled in Jesus' disciples.

As a prophecy of Christ Himself, Amos 9:11–12 is referring to
the exaltation of Christ, His resurrection from the dead and ascension. The promise that Yahweh would "raise up" David's booth
employs a resurrection image, and this point is strengthened when
we recognize that the pronoun in the third clause of verse 11 ("I will
also raise up his ruins") refers back to David. Ruined David, Amos
predicts, will be raised. Jesus, who tabernacled among us, was
thrown down in death, but the fallen tabernacle will be raised.
Given the royal connotations of the "tent of David" in Isaiah 16:5,
moreover, Amos's prophecy includes a promise of a restored Davidic
ruler. When Jesus ascended to take the throne at the Father's right
hand, He fulfilled completely what was pictured in David's enthronement in the ark-shrine (2 Sam. 7:18). Jesus is both the restored booth, and the one who sits as judge within it (Is. 16:5).

And the booth is also Jesus' body. That is to say, "tent of David"
is one of the many images or types of the church in Scripture. Those
who are in Christ also form a temple/tabernacle with Him, and so
the tabernacle of David is a suitable symbol for the people of God.
To say that the church is the temple of God is to say that she is the
dwelling of the Spirit, a holy people, consisting of living stones. One
can also say that the church is the Davidic tabernacle, but the force

[19] Dupont, "Je rebâtirai la cabane de David," 22.

of that image moves in a different direction: the church is the Davidic tabernacle because she offers open access to all, because she is an undivided tent, because she is a joyful throng engaged in song, and because Gentiles are incorporated. At some level, it is most certainly true that the church is both temple and Davidic tabernacle.

True as these perspectives are, they do not do justice to the temporal sequence that we find in Samuel. In addition to seeing "Davidic tent" and "Solomon's temple" both fulfilled in Christ and His church, we must try to see how the temporal sequence from David's tent (or, more exactly, from a divided sanctuary) to Solomon's temple provides a typological preview of the New Covenant. Below I offer several tentative proposals, some of which are more convincing and fruitful than others.

1. If I am correct about the features of the Davidic tent—especially the freedom of access and the Gentile incorporation—the temple of Solomon seems like a reversion. Not even the priests were allowed to enter the Most Holy Place of the temple, but apparently David and the Levites were permitted to enter the Davidic tent. After coming to an eschatological high point, a moment of fulfilled promise, it seems that Israel took a step backward and came under the Law. Solomon comes off looking like a Judaizer.

That is not, however, fatal to the argument presented in this book. After all, this pattern of promise, Law, and fulfilled promise is common in Scripture. Long before Aaron became priest, Melchizedek received tithes from Abraham (Gen. 14:20; Heb. 7:4–9), and during the time of the Aaronic priesthood, Yahweh held out the promise of a restored Melchizedekan priesthood (Ps. 110:4; Heb. 7:11–28). Thus, the pattern in the history of the priesthood was Melchizedek, Aaron, and then the new Melchizedek, and this matched the pattern in the history of the sanctuary: undivided Davidic tent, divided Solomonic temple, and undivided heavenly tabernacle.[20] We could

---

[20] This is also similar to the promise-law-fulfillment pattern in Galatians 3. The Lord gave the promise to Abraham first, and the promise set out the agenda for God's work in history. From that time, He intended to bless the Gentiles through Abraham's seed. Even when the

paraphrase Hebrews 7:11 in this way: "If perfection came through the temple of Solomon, what further need was there for a promise that David's booth would be raised?"

The underlying logic of this arrangement would be that God provided a preview of the eschatological order at an initial stage, and then established a sub-eschatological order as a means for achieving the final goal. The beginning of the end is not followed by the end; the end of the end comes much later. Melchizedek provided a preview of the future priest, and the Aaronic priesthood was a means toward the end of a future Melchizedekan priesthood. The Davidic tent was a type of the eschatological sanctuary, and the temple provided a mechanism for reaching that goal. Implicit in this formulation is the conclusion that the restoration of the earlier Davidic system was always the underlying or overriding hope for Israel. All the while the Aaronic priests ministered in the temple, Israel was to be hoping for Melchizedek; all the while Israel was performing sacrifice at the first and second temples, they were to hope for a time when the sacrifice of praise would again dominate their worship; all the while Israel was focused on Moriah, they were to be hoping for a new Zion.[21]

2. The previous analysis of the typology assumes that David's ark-shrine on Zion was the beginning point of a progression of sanctuaries, and that Amos's prophecy covers the entire New Covenant order. If we maintain the first assumption, but dispense with the second, we can see analogies between the "tent-temple" sequence and other two-stage constructions in Scripture:

---

Law with its regulations and restrictions was added 430 years later, the Abrahamic promise remained in force. The law was a means for fulfilling the promise, rather than the promise being a means for establishing Israel under the law; the law as a system of worship and national life was always temporary, and this was clear because the promise preceded it. Thus the promise—Law—fulfilled promise sequence matches the access—restricted access—access sequence with regard to the sanctuary.

[21] If this is right, the wickedness of Israel's treatment of Gentiles as unclean and abominable becomes all the more apparent. For the prophetic promise that Zion would rise again was a constant reminder that the future would see myriads of Obed-edoms.

| *Exodus* | *David* | *Restoration* | *New Testament* |
|---|---|---|---|
| Tent in wilderness (or, Moses' tent) | Ark in Zion | Altar | Apostolic |
| 40 years | 40 years | 20 years | 40 years |
| Tent in Shiloh | Solomon's temple | Second temple | Post-70 church |

In each case, the first sanctuary was temporary and was replaced by a more permanent and more glorious order of things. From this perspective, Amos's prophecy is specifically a prophecy of the apostolic period and would be particularly relevant in some way to the issues before the church at the Jerusalem council.[22]

3. Let's see what happens when we assume that the ark-shrine was neither the beginning nor the endpoint of a new progression, but rather a turning point in a larger sequence. From this perspective, the story of the sanctuary is as follows: The Mosaic tabernacle is rent in two at Aphek and remains divided through the reign of Saul; during the reign of David, however, the main portion of the tabernacle, the Lord's ark-throne, ascends to Jerusalem, and this is marked as an event of cosmic and eschatological significance because it is the first time Yahweh has ever dwelt in His city; yet, this is only the beginning of the end of the story, because the sanctuary is still divided; finally, the ark moves into the temple, the remainder of the tabernacle furnishings (and some new ones) are brought into Jerusalem, and this reunited sanctuary comes to be called "Zion." Or, more simply, the story is of division of the tabernacle, ascension of one portion to its permanent place, and then reunion.

This analysis opens up a number of intriguing analogies. First, the story of the sanctuary recapitulates in history the ritual of the

---

[22] In this respect, the fact that the apostolic church was concerned with the incorporation of Gentile God-fearers is relevant. David did not incorporate utter pagans into the worship at his tabernacle; Obed-edom was already a Gentile God-fearer before He became a Levitical musician or gatekeeper. Similarly, Amos promised that the restoration of David's tent would involve the possession of Edom, the brother-nation to Israel, descended from Esau. And in the apostolic church, the question had to do mainly with the incorporation of already observant Gentiles into the community of the church. Cornelius certainly was a God-fearer long before Peter ever met him (Acts 10:1ff). Amos's prophecy and its fulfillment thus had particular relevance to the situation of the first century.

ascension offering. Just as the animal is killed and dismembered (Lev. 1:5–6), so the tabernacle is torn apart. After the priests have arranged the wood on the altar, the head and fat are placed on the fire and begin to ascend in smoke (1:8), and this would correspond to the ascension of the ark to Jerusalem. Once the head has been placed on the altar, the remainder of the animal is burned, particularly the entrails (1:9). In this way, the entire animal is transfigured into smoke, as the dismembered pieces of the tabernacle were transfigured into the reunited temple of Solomon.

Along similar lines, we can see the story of the tabernacle's "death and resurrection" as a type of the death and resurrection of the *totus Christus*. The tabernacle was, among other things, an architectural presentation of the human body, and in this representation, the Most Holy Place and the ark corresponded to the human head.[23] Thus, the rending of the Mosaic tabernacle not only corresponded to the sacrifice of an animal, but pointed to the tearing apart of a man. Once the tabernacle-man was torn, his "head" (i.e., the ark and the Most Holy Place) ascended to Zion. Later, the rest of the body joined the head in Jerusalem, and the head ascended to the more glorious house of the temple. This is a typological preview of the work of Jesus: He was torn on Calvary, and as the Ark-Head he ascended to heaven. The cosmic imagery associated with the ascension of the ark in 1 Chronicles 16 thus points to the ascension of Jesus to the heavenly throne and tent. In a sense, the body also ascended with Him (Eph. 2:6), but in a specific sense the ascension of the body took place only at the end of the apostolic period, when Jerusalem was destroyed and the saints of the firstfruits church "came to life and reigned with Christ a thousand years" (Rev. 20:4). After that, the church that had been in "Gibeon" joined the Ark in "Zion" in a glorious temple.

Another aspect of this typology may be noted. Gethsemane can be seen as the point where Christ's body was torn. Threatened by

---

[23] See James B. Jordan, *Through New Eyes: Developing a Biblical View of the World* (Eugene, Ore.: Wipf & Stock, 1999), 216–217; Vern Poythress, *The Shadow of Christ in the Law of Moses* (Brentwood, Tenn.: Wolgemuth & Hyatt, 1991), 53–54.

the Jews, Jesus' disciples—His limbs—fled from Him, and that
separation was a division of the body of Christ. "Destroy this
temple" refers not only to the temple of His physical body, but the
temple of His corporate body.[24] After the booth of David was raised
up in the resurrection, the rest of the body was reunited with the
exalted Head.

The tabernacle of Moses also had a corporate dimension. It was
an architectural man, but it was also an architectural representation
of Israel. From this perspective, the division of the Mosaic tent fore-
shadows the division of the nation after Solomon, and the exile
points to Israel's Babylonian captivity. The placement of the ark on
Zion corresponds to the restoration from exile, the beginning of the
end, when a remnant of Israel regathered in Jerusalem and erected
the temple. But this "beginning of return" was not the final return
from exile, which awaited the coming of Messiah.[25] More precisely,
the initial return awaited the Lord's designation of the place for His
permanent house, which He marked by fire at Pentecost. At that
point, fire fell from heaven to show that this people, the disciples
of Jesus, were the new temple, the new location where sacrifices of
praise were to be offered.

Finally, the division of worship during David's reign perhaps pre-
views the division that existed among the people of God during the
apostolic period. Throughout the New Testament, Jewish Christians worshiped at the temple (e.g., Lk. 24:50–53) and even offered
sacrifice (e.g., Acts 21:26), even though they knew the temple and
its worship were fulfilled in Christ and ultimately doomed. Gentiles who became believers were not, however, required to come
under the Law that governed Jewish temple-worshipers, but instead
worshiped in homes, offering not animal sacrifices but the "sacrifice of praise." This situation of divided worship lasted a generation,
until Jew and Gentile had been knit together into one new man,
worshiping together in an undivided temple, the temple that is the
church of Christ.

---

[24] I owe this suggestion to Mark Horne's lectures on Mark.

[25] This two-stage return from exile provides a nuance on N. T. Wright's thesis that first-
century Israel was "still in exile."

# 6

# The Ends of Song

Reformed liturgics has been known for centuries for its adherence to what is known as the "regulative principle of worship." In its simple formulation, this principle states that "whatever is not commanded in Scripture is forbidden in worship," or, more loosely, that liturgical practices must be based on Scripture. There is, however, considerable disagreement about how this principle is to work in practice. This is not the place to enter into the strengths and weaknesses of the different formulas. Instead, I want to suggest that the material from Chronicles reviewed in this book offers helpful perspectives on these issues. For the record, let me say that I do not believe that the strict formula quoted above is scriptural, and for that reason I do not find it practicable. I adhere to the regulative principle in the sense that we are to worship God as He has taught us to worship Him, but He has taught us in myriads of ways, and not merely in explicit commands. As I will attempt to show, the example of David supports my viewpoint against the "strict regulativists." Perhaps I will be accused of offering a caricature of my opponents. If that is so, I hope it is the right kind of caricature, the kind that is as recognizable as a photograph.

In this chapter, I address two main areas of concern. The first has to do with liturgical hermeneutics, i.e., How are Christians to apply Scripture to our worship? In the second main section,

I examine some features of the theology of liturgical music found
in Chronicles.

## Regulation By Analogy

As we saw in chapter 4, David applied the Mosaic law when he
appointed the Levites for their ministry of music at the ark-shrine
and at the temple. That discussion raises two large issues of liturgical theology and practice. First, it raises the question of liturgical
hermeneutics, of how we are to apply the Bible to worship. From
the Law, David learned that Levites were chosen to "minister" to
Yahweh, and he concluded that this ministry legitimately included
song. Kleinig suggests that David was applying the following line
of reasoning:

> The temporary responsibility of the Levites for the transportation of the ark
> was part of a larger and more permanent duty to minister to the Lord who
> sat enthroned above it and met with his people there. This ministry, which
> was performed "in" or "with the Lord's name" (Deut. 18.5, 7), was carried
> out by the Levites as they proclaimed that name to the people in songs of
> praise. So then, while liturgical song was not explicitly instituted in the
> Pentateuch, it was held to be included in the commission of the Levites by
> the Lord to minister in his name.[1]

Elsewhere, Kleinig helpfully suggests that there was an analogy
between "kings in the ancient world [who] were entertained with
music and song in their banquets" and the ministry of music to a
god,[2] and this perhaps provides another insight into the logic of
David's application of the Law. Yahweh's altar was His "table" and
the sacrifices are His "bread" (e.g., Lev. 21:16–24). Thus, Levitical
"ministry" or "service" was "table service." David expanded *sharat* to
include musical performance by reasoning that Yahweh should be
served at His table as a king would be served at his, with a banquet
of song to accompany the banquet of flesh, bread, and wine.

---

[1] Kleinig, *The Lord's Song: The Basis, Function and Significance of Choral Music in
Chronicles* (*JSOT* Supplement #156; Sheffield: *JSOT* Press, 1993), 34.

[2] Ibid., 100.

Similarly, as noted in chapter 4, David expanded the Mosaic requirement of trumpets at the daily ascensions (Num. 10:9–10) to include other sorts of musical "memorials." David's reasoning at this point seems fairly straightforward: if trumpets must be blown over the ascensions and communion sacrifices, then other musical instruments are legitimate for worship as well, even if they are not explicitly required in the Law. Kleinig speculates about a further element in David's application of Numbers 10:

> By sounding the trumpets the priests were to proclaim the Lord's presence and announce that he had come to the aid of his people. But the trumpets could not by themselves announce the Lord's presence. Indeed, how else could his presence be announced but by mention of his name, which was his "mode of remembrance" (Exod. 3.15)? The trumpet was therefore supplemented by the instruments used to accompany those sacred songs which were sung to introduce the Lord by name. The whole temple choir, which consisted of priestly trumpeters and Levitical musicians, thus announced the Lord and proclaimed his presence. The divine command of Num. 10.10 was thereby fulfilled by David through the institution of the choral rite.[3]

If Kleinig is correct, then the Law's demands could not be obeyed fully without David's addition of choral music. Worship that included *only* trumpets could not clearly and fully memorialize Yahweh's name. David, in short, was not merely thinking, "The Law is fine as it is, but we can incorporate new means of worship that are consistent with the Law, or analogous to the Law's requirements, in order to glorify and adorn worship." Rather, he was thinking, "If I do only what the Law requires, I cannot completely obey the Law. To fulfill the Law, I must have a righteousness that surpasses the scribes and Pharisees."

Whether or not this last point reflects David's actual intentions, it is clear that David did not see the absence of musical ministry in the Mosaic Law as a reason to prohibit musical ministry. Rather, he interpreted and applied the Mosaic Law as requiring (or, at least, permitting) musical ministry. Clearly, he was operating by some sort

[3] Ibid., 36–37.

of regulative principle of worship, since he cited the Law as grounds
for the worship he instituted, but just as clearly he was not operating with a wooden and rigid form of the regulative principle. A strict
regulativist living at the time of David would syllogize thus:

> Major premise: Whatever is not commanded is forbidden.
> Minor premise: Singing is not commanded in the Levitical Law.
> Conclusion: Therefore, singing in worship is forbidden.

David appears to have reasoned by analogy:

> Major premise: The Law governs worship.
> Minor premise #1: The Law prescribes that trumpets be played over the public
>     ascensions, in public worship.
> Minor premise #2: The trumpet is a musical instrument.
> Conclusion: Analogously, song and other music are a legitimate part of
>     worship.[4]

David's example gives us a canonical illustration of liturgical interpretation and application of the Mosaic law, and it shows that
the liturgical use of the law in the Old Testament itself was not at
all wooden and rigid.[5] In place of a "regulation-by-explicit command" principle, David operated according to a "regulation-by-
analogy" principle.

Of course, not all analogies are legitimate. David could not reason:

> Major Premise: God demands animal sacrifices.
> Minor Premise: A pig is an animal.
> Conclusion: We may legitimately offer pigs in sacrifice.

That analogy runs contrary to the explicit commands of the Law.
Nor could he reason from, say, the liturgical blowing of trumpets

---

[4] An analogy between musical instruments and "voiced" human beings may also be at work.
Certainly, the Bible points to an analogy between the temple vessels, including the musical
instruments, and human beings.

[5] Of course, such regulativists would not criticize David, since they would point out that
David had new revelation from God that gave warrant to introduce these innovations. As we
have seen, however, the Chronicler was at pains to show that this new revelation was an application and expansion of the Mosaic ordinances, not a completely new form.

to the liturgical blowing of one's nose. Analogies have to be governed by the explicit statements of Scripture, and by common sense governed by Scripture.

Yet, a "regulation-by-analogy" provides concrete and scriptural guidance on a host of specific liturgical questions. It is not a "squishy" principle that can justify anything that might enter our heads. For example, Scripture does not command the church to put a tablecloth or candles on the Lord's table. For a strict regulativist, this ends the discussion; no candles or tablecloths may be used. Reasoning by analogy, however, we must ask what kind of event is taking place at the Lord's table, and the scriptural answer is that the church is feeding on Christ and enjoying a foretaste of the heavenly banquet, the marriage Supper of the Lamb. Given that analogy, adornments like tablecloths and candles are perfectly legitimate; they are consistent with the analogy—the *scriptural* analogy—between the Lord's Supper and a wedding feast. By contrast, a bare table without any adornment does not communicate the fact that the Supper is a wedding feast. But that is what Scripture says the meal *is*. Removing the candles and the tablecloth changed the meaning of a divinely established sacrament; instead of a feast it became a fast, a slab in the morgue rather than a table. Reasoning by analogy, therefore, we arrive at the conclusion that adornments are not only legitimate, but demanded by the nature of the event. Were I being frisky, I could turn all the strict regulativists texts against them; they are the ones offering strange fire because the bare unadorned table *violates* Scripture.

"Squishy"? I don't think so. Analogists can thunder with the best of them.

## Leviticus and Christian Liturgy

A second large set of implications has to do with the relevance of the Old Testament sacrificial system to Christian liturgy. For a number of years, several Reformed liturgists—especially the "Biblical Horizons group" that includes James B. Jordan, Jeffrey M.

Meyers, and myself—have been arguing that the Levitical system provides a great deal of instruction for both the theology and practice of Christian worship. A number of arguments in defense of this effort may be offered. For myself the main argument is, What is the alternative? Where else do we go, if we are going to be Biblical, to work out the meaning of worship? What book gives us more information about worship than Leviticus? Certainly, no book of the New Testament offers anything like a theology of worship, or even much practical guidance. Reformed liturgists who limit themselves to the New Testament are practicing dispensationalists, however strongly their professed adherence to covenant theology. And, though certain isolated "elements" of worship can be teased out of the New Testament, little is said about the order or significance of these elements. Liturgists who refuse to turn to Leviticus operate with a thin liturgical theology, assume an atomistic view of liturgical practice, and often rely heavily on extra-biblical Jewish and Christian tradition to work out the details of worship.

Another argument in favor of using the sacrificial texts is historical. Christianity, of course, first took root among Jews, a people that had been worshiping according to the regulations of Leviticus (modified by David, as we have seen) for a millennium and a half. Those centuries of reflection on the Mosaic legislation, and practice of sacrifice, provided the framework for their understanding of Christian worship. When Hebrews 13 said that we are to offer a "sacrifice of praise, the fruit of our lips," those words were not uttered in a liturgical and theological vacuum; the mind of the first-century Jew would no doubt go immediately to his experience as a worshiper in the temple and synagogue.[6] When Peter said that Christians form a royal priesthood for offering spiritual sacrifice, that too was inevitably understood in the context of Jewish worship. When Jesus called the Lord's Supper "My memorial," He was using a term

---

[6] There are hints that synagogue worship developed as a transformation of the sacrificial worship of the temple. For some details, see my "Synagogue or Temple? Models of Christian Worship," *Westminster Theological Journal* (forthcoming).

that the Jews would have associated with their sacrificial system. In purely historical terms, if we want to understand the *New* Testament's descriptions of worship, we are forced to examine the *Old* Testament worship.

One of the particular claims of this school of Reformed liturgics is that the sacrificial system provides us with a rudimentary order of worship that can be applied to Christian worship.[7] The argument can be made in several ways. First, the ritual of each animal offering prescribes a sequence of actions that culminates with union and communion with Yahweh:

> Animal presented for offering
> Worshiper leans on head of animal
> Worshiper slaughters the animal
> Priest presents blood on the altar
> Priest arranges flesh on the altar
> Animal's flesh turns to smoke on the altar
> Worshiper (sometimes) receives a portion of the flesh in a meal[8]

Translated into the terms of Christian worship, this provides the following sequence:

> Worshipers gather
> Worshipers invoke Christ as their representative and substitute (leaning hand)
> Worshipers confess sins, hear absolution (slaughter and blood)
> Worshipers ascend to God, hear His Word, sing His praises (burning)
> Worshipers eat a sacrificial meal

Or, more simply, each offering moves through the sequence of confession and cleansing, consecration, and communion, and so does Christian worship.

---

[7] See James B. Jordan, *Theses on Worship: Notes Toward the Reformation of Worship* (Niceville, Fla.: Transfiguration Press, 1994), 93–104; Jeffrey Meyers, *The Lord's Service: Worship at Providence Reformed Presbyterian Church* (unpublished), 17–29, 112–122.

[8] For a discussion of the significance of these various actions, see my *A House for My Name: A Survey of the Old Testament* (Moscow: Canon, 2000), 89–92. For a very detailed discussion, see J. H. Kurtz, *Offerings, Sacrifices and Worship in the Old Testament* (trans. James Martin; Peabody, Mass.: Hendrickson, 1998).

The same sequence is evident in the order of sacrifices when more than one offering is made. In the passages that describe the sequence of offerings, the order is fairly standard. If a purification is made at all, it is offered first; this is followed by an ascension; and a communion sacrifice or peace offering concludes the sequence. This sequence is found in full in two fairly specialized rituals: the ordination of priests (Exod. 29:10–34; Lev. 8:14–29) and the related reconsecration rite for a Nazirite who has been defiled by a dead body (Num. 6:16–17). In a number of large-scale public celebrations, the same sequence is found. Hezekiah's rededication of the temple began with purifications, moved through ascensions, and culminated with sacrifices and thank offerings (2 Chr. 29:20–36).[9] The sequence of ascension-communion is built into the sacrificial system, since ascensions were offered by the priests every morning and evening (Num. 28:1–8), and every peace offering during the day would be added to the "continual" ascension. On certain feast days, moreover, a purification offering was added to the public rite (Num. 29:1–38), and these preceded the offering of the daily ascension and the festival sacrifices.[10]

The fundamental claim here is that sacrificial worship did not cease with the coming of the New Covenant, but was transformed into a "spiritual sacrifice" and "sacrifice of praise." We now do different things than ancient Israelites did, but those actions have the same meaning as the actions in the Levitical ceremonies. We no longer slaughter bulls and goats for blood purification, but we do confess our sins so as to be cleansed (1 Jn. 1:8–9). We no longer dismember animals before the Lord's table, but instead the Word cuts us into pieces so that we may be offered as sacrifices (Heb. 4:11–12). We no longer keep Passover but we celebrate the Lord's Supper, which fulfills Passover (among other things) and may be

---

[9] "Thank offerings" are a form of peace offering, according to Lev. 7:15–18.

[10] Admittedly, the priority of the purification is not explicitly stated, but any other order is senseless. The purification prepared the altar and tabernacle for sacrifice, and it would be absurd to place it after other offerings. Of course, if only an ascension is being offered, the blood of the ascension is sufficient.

described as a Christian Passover. This same "transposition" from an Old to a New Covenant key can be applied to other rituals of the Levitical system. We understand what we are doing in worship through the categories of the sacrificial system, under the metaphor of sacrifice.

Not everyone is convinced that the sequence of sacrifices provides an authoritative pattern for Christian worship. While praising James Jordan's liturgical work for its creativity, John Frame is skeptical that we can derive "strict rules for the order of worship" from "symbolism."[11] Though it may be insufficient to convince Prof. Frame, the texts concerned with Davidic worship support Jordan's (and others') use of symbols and patterns from Leviticus. In the Davidic system as described by Chronicles, we find an example—a *canonical* example, mind you—of a similar process of transformation. As noted above, David cited the Mosaic sacrificial law to give warrant to worship that heavily emphasized music rather than animal offering. In the terminological discussion in chapter 4, we noted that the sacrificial terms are employed to describe Davidic worship in a number of respects. Like the burned portion of a tribute offering, music was a "memorial"; when the Levites played instruments and sang they were "standing to serve" as the law required; their divisions were described as "watches," and their singing was considered a new form of "labor," analogous to the transport of the tabernacle during the Mosaic period. In short, we see already in David's time the Old Testament origins of the idea of a "sacrifice of praise," and Chronicles shows that this notion grows out of an application of sacrificial law. This example gives us plenty of warrant to explore how other aspects of Levitical ceremony might guide the theology and practice of Christian worship.

But that task must be left for a later day, or never.

## A New Song

The theology of worship music in Chronicles is largely implicit in the way that the Chronicler applies the terminology of sacrifice

---

[11] *Worship in Spirit and Truth* (Philipsburg, N.J.: P&R, 1996), 158.

to the offering of musical worship. A number of specific dimensions of liturgical music will be explored below. In many cases, my
discussion is no more than suggestive, offering hints and clues that
could well be expanded greatly. On a few points, I attempt to apply the discussion to specific issues in liturgical debate, but I am for
the most part content to leave detailed application to those sufficiently competent in music to draw sane conclusions. Though I
believe there is a place for trained musicians in the church, I assume
throughout that the church as a whole is the fulfillment of the Levitical musicians.[12]

1. **Music as "Song."** According to the terminology of Scripture,
"song" (*shir*) covers both instrumental and vocal music. A sharp distinction between them is thus foreign to scriptural categories.
Though the fact that Hebrew has no separate term for instrumental music does not *prove* that they were incapable of distinguishing
choral from instrumental music, it should cause some hesitation
among those who would erect a sharp distinction between them.
This, of course, is precisely what many Reformed liturgists have
done. The entire argument against instrumental music assumes that
"instrumental music" is a distinct ethical and liturgical category; but
this is precisely what the biblical terminology seems to deny. The
close connection between choral and temporal music is reflected also
in the theology of temple vessels. As James B. Jordan has pointed
out, the temple vessels represented the people of Israel, devoted to
the service of Yahweh; when Israel went into exile, the vessels were
taken as well. After David's time, these "vessels" (*keli*) included
musical instruments, and these too represented the people of Israel.
Men are voiced instruments of worship, and music from instruments is analogous to human singing.

Another aspect of the traditional argument against liturgical instruments is that the temple service was purely typological and ab-
rogated in the New Covenant. Nothing distinctive to the temple

---

[12] For an argument along these lines pertaining to the priesthood, see my *Priesthood of the
Plebs: The Baptismal Transformation of Antique Order* (Eugene, Ore.: Wipf & Stock, forthcoming).

worship—animal sacrifices, a consecrated priesthood, and musical instruments—should be introduced into Christian worship. To do so is to become a Judaizer.[13] The discussion of the last few pages, however, shows that this is simply a mistake. True, the temple worship is no longer performed as it was in the second temple period, but temple worship is still being performed in a different manner. The one main area of literal continuity between the two is in the area of music, and temple music was always performed with instrumental accompaniment. Indeed, Scripture contains *no* examples of unaccompanied singing. Instrumental music in worship is perfectly admissible, and even prescribed.[14]

Consideration of the prophecy of Amos 9 leads to the same conclusion. However we understand the typology of the Davidic tabernacle, it is clear that the apostolic church saw itself as the fulfillment of the Davidic sanctuary. It is impossible that they should understand themselves as the fulfillment of the Davidic period and of Amos's prophecy of a renewed Davidic tent, and conclude that the instrumental music that was associated with the Davidic tent was illicit. If Israel burst into song when Yahweh came to dwell on the typological Zion, how much more when Jesus, the Incarnate Yahweh, ascends to heavenly Zion. If the beginning of the end is marked by trumpets and cymbals, how much more the end of the beginning.

---

[13] John Girardeau's treatise against instrumental music is still cited in Reformed circles and is currently available at www.fpcr.org. Girardeau's argument rests on his claim that the temple service was typological while the synagogue service provides a practical model for Christian worship. He recognizes that the worship of Israel's temple embodied certain permanent liturgical forms, but also argues that the temple worship was infused with temporary and typological features. By contrast, "no element of synagogue worship was typical and temporary," a point he claims is "too evident to require argument." Thus, the "specific difference between [synagogue and temple worship] lay in the possession by one of the accidental and temporary, and the non-possession by the other of the same." To isolate these typological elements of the temple worship with this formula: (elements of temple service) - (elements of synagogue worship) = (typological elements of temple worship). For more, see my article "Synagogue or Temple?"

[14] Again, friskily, we might point out that the strict regulativists are the ones out of accord with Scripture.

2. The "King's Song." The Chronicler shows the Levitical choir and orchestra performed their worship "under the hand" of David, that is, under his authority (1 Chr. 25:2). More strongly, 2 Chronicles 7:6 indicates that David actually praised Yahweh *through* the ministrations of the Levites:

> And the priests stood at their posts and the Levites, with the instruments of praise to Yahweh, which King David had made for giving praise to Yahweh—"for His lovingkindness is everlasting"—whenever David gave praise by their hand, while the priests on the other side blew trumpets, and all Israel was standing.

On the one hand, the musicians performed "under the hand" of David; on the other hand, David himself praised Yahweh "by their hand."[15] Levitical praise is the King's Song before his "Father," even if it is performed by Levites. And it was David's song even though David was not present. As Kleinig points out, this passage is particularly striking because it describes the dedication of the temple, which took place after the completion of the temple and (apparently) after the construction of Solomon's house. The latter was finished in the twenty-fourth year of Solomon (1 Kgs. 6:38–7:1). Thus, 2 Chronicles 7:6 speaks of David's participation in praise, even though he had been dead for over two decades.[16]

All of this suggests a profound typology of worship music. On earth, Jesus joined with His disciples in praise to His heavenly Father (e.g., Mt. 26:30), and now He has been exalted to *receive* the praise of the angelic choirs. As the Lamb that was slain, He sits enthroned before living creatures who declare His worthiness and power (Rev. 5:1–14). Yet, Jesus has not ceased to offer praise to His Father. As Hebrews says, Jesus is the speaker in Psalm 22:22: "I will proclaim Thy name to My brethren, in the midst of the congregation I will

[15] Possibly, the phrase refers to cheironomy, musical direction through a kind of sign language. But for the Chronicler the phrase "under the hand of" also connotes "under the authority of" (see 2 Chr. 21:10; 26:11; 31:13).

[16] *The Lord's Song*, 92–93. The NIV translates this clause: "which King David had made for praising the LORD and which were used when he gave thanks," thus suggesting that the Chronicler is referring back to the reign of David.

sing Thy praise" (Heb. 2:12). Gathered for worship, united in song, the body of Christ, along with the Head, *is* Christ offering praise to His Father. The Greater David gives praise by *our* hand.

3. **Seeking God in Song.** The theme of "seeking" God is prominent in the Chronicler's account of the ark. Saul lost the kingdom because he sought out a medium instead of seeking the counsel of Yahweh (1 Chr. 10:13–14), and Saul's failure to seek God is linked with his failure to seek the ark. Once he became king, David urged Israel to bring "the ark of our God to us, for we did not seek it in the days of Saul" (13:3). In seeking the ark of God, David is seeking God Himself, and thus reversing the failure of Saul's reign. Merely seeking God any old way would not do, however, as David discovered when he first attempted to bring the ark to Zion. David later recognized that Yahweh's wrath broke out against Israel because "we did not seek Him according to the ordinance" (15:13). Israel's liturgical law was designed to mark out a pathway for seeking God; by obedience to the ordinance, Israel would be brought into near communion with Yahweh. After the temple was built, any Israelites who "set their hearts on seeking Yahweh God of Israel" could go "to Jerusalem to sacrifice to Yahweh God of their fathers" (2 Chr. 11:16).[17]

In several ways, Chronicles indicates that song was a means for seeking God. David's transport of the ark to Jerusalem was a way of "seeking Yahweh" (1 Chr. 15:13), and the effort to "seek God" did not end when the ark rested in David's tent. Rather, at David's tent, the Levites urged the people in the midst of their song to "seek Yahweh and His strength; seek His face continually" (16:11). How were they to seek His face at Zion? Since the worship at Zion was predominantly musical, the answer is evident. They were to seek the Lord's face in the way that the Levites directed—in song. Moreover, David emphasized that seeking God must be done "according to the ordinance" (15:13). In context, "ordinance" refers to the Mosaic law that required Levites to carry the ark, but elsewhere we learn that

---

[17] For a discussion of related passages, see ibid., 30–31.

David also enforced "ordinances" for worship (e.g., 2 Chr. 8:14), and these required the Levites to sing. "After David's day, therefore, seeking Yahweh "according to the ordinance" meant seeking Him in song. Finally, the Chronicler's account of the liturgical battle of Jehoshaphat indicates that this musical performance was part of the king's effort to "seek Yahweh." At the beginning of the account, we learn that Jehoshaphat refused to "seek the Baals" but instead "sought the God of his father" (2 Chr. 17:3–4) and he is commended for this (19:3). At the climax of his reign, when the Moabites and Meunites began to threaten Judah, he again "set his face to seek Yahweh" and called Judah together "to seek help from Yahweh" (20:3–4). This effort to "seek Yahweh's help" took the form of prayer and song, during which Yahweh scattered the Moabites and drove them away.

In this sense, every Christian must submit to the regulative principle of worship, for those who seek God find Him if they seek Him according to the ordinance. All who worship Him must worship Him according to truth.

4. **Song as Memorial.** As discussed in chapter 4, the Chronicler refers to music as a way of memorializing the Lord's name. The first "memorial" in Scripture was the rainbow, which was set in the cloud to remind Yahweh of His promise: "And it shall come about, when I bring a cloud over the earth, that the bow shall be seen in the cloud, and I will remember My covenant, which is between Me and you and every living creature of all flesh; and never again shall the water become a flood to destroy all flesh" (Gen. 9:14–15). Several ceremonies in the sacrificial law are also called "memorials." A handful of the tribute offering was offered up in smoke "as its memorial portion on the altar" (Lev. 2:2, 9, 16; Heb. *'azkarat*), and a handful of the purification offering of grain, which was offered by the poor, was offered on the altar as its "memorial portion" (Lev. 5:12; Heb. *'azkarat*). Though the word "memorial" is not used to describe the animal offerings, the portions burned on the altar seem to have a similar purpose; they ascend as a reminder of Yahweh's promise

to grant forgiveness and to accept the worshiper through the animal offered.[18]

How does song serve as a memorial? Evidently, we have an example of such memorizing in the psalm recorded in 1 Chronicles 16:8–36. Of course, this psalm is also an illustration of Levitical "thanks" and "praise" (see 16:4); it begins with an exhortation to "give thanks to Yahweh" and to "sing praises to Him" (16:8–9), and ends on the same note (vv. 34–36). Yet, the psalm is also a "memorial" psalm. That is, it is a psalm that reminds Yahweh of His promises and of His great deeds in the past; it "causes Him to remember." Israel is exhorted to "remember His wonderful deeds which He has done" and to "remember His covenant forever" (vv. 12, 15), and Yahweh Himself is told of His covenant with Abraham, His protection of Israel during her years of weakness, His "wonderful deeds among all the peoples," and His work of creation (vv. 16–17, 21, 24, 30). In retelling the promises and works of God, the psalm is simultaneously calling on Him to do the same again. When Yahweh "remembers" His covenant, He acts to deliver His people. Song ascends to bring His promises to His remembrance.[19] When Yahweh opens His eyes, He sees through the rainbow, and remembers His covenant; when he opens His ears, he hears the song of His people, and draws near to deliver.[20]

The fact that psalm-singing is an act of memorializing the work of God holds important implications for our understanding of

---

[18] It is possible that grain offerings are somehow peculiarly memorials in a way that animal offerings are not. This might have some implications for the theology of the eucharistic memorial. Also, though I am stressing the Godward direction of memorials, I am not denying that memorials also speak to men. Thus, the rainbow reminds the Lord of His promise, but when we see the rainbow, we should be reminded that the Lord is reminded, and that should increase our assurance and confidence in Him.

[19] This was a particularly apt note to strike with the Chronicler's original post-exilic readership, for Israel had again become "few in number, very few, and strangers" in the land, wandering "from nation to nation, and from one kingdom to another people" (vv. 19–20).

[20] This provides biblical support for singing creeds. Singing the creed is a wonderful pedagogical tool, but it is also directed heavenward: the creed memorializes the Lord's works as Creator and Redeemer, and when sung before Him calls on Him to respond and act again on our behalf.

worship music. First, it provides an argument against exclusive psalmody. When Israel came out of Egypt, Miriam led the women in a song of praise for the Lord's deliverance (Exod. 15:1–21). Since the Exodus was the most recent deliverance, that was the focus of the musical memorial. When Deborah composed her psalm, she too referred to the events surrounding the exodus (Judg. 5:5), but the focus of her psalm was on the deliverance from Jabin king of Canaan that had only recently been achieved (especially vv. 19–31). Thus, Deborah memorialized not only the distant past, but the recent past. The same, of course, is true of the psalms in the book of Psalms, which not only dwell on the original deliverance of Israel from Egypt, but also celebrate and memorialize Yahweh's mercies to David and others. This pattern indicates that liturgical song should remind our Father not only of what He has done long ago, but of what He has recently done. Thus, it seems perfectly nonsensical to suggest that no hymn can be sung in worship that recounts the events of Christ's life, death, and resurrection. This is especially the case since Jesus is the New Covenant memorial name of God.

If liturgical song is a "memorial," secondly, it is in an important sense directed toward God. He is the "audience" addressed in liturgical song, the One who is being reminded of His promises and actions, the recipient of praise and thanks. Just as sacrificial smoke ascends to the Lord's presence, so sacrificial sounds arises to heaven, and "He who made the ear, does He not hear?" What this means in detail I do not presume to know; but it at least means that our tastes, or the need to communicate to unbelievers, cannot be the overriding standard of the substance or style of worship music. Since our Father is the audience of song, His musical tastes must be determined and determinative.

5. **Song and Yahweh's glory.** We can understand song more fully as "seeking God" and as "memorial" when we examine the connection between song and the glory of Yahweh. The Chronicler's account of the dedication of Solomon's temple repeats the scene of the dedication of the Mosaic tabernacle. Both occur after a sanctuary has

been completed. In both, priests are consecrated (Exod. 40:12–16; 2 Chr. 5:11), sacrifices are offered (Exod. 40:29; 2 Chr. 5:6), and furniture was moved in (Exod. 40:20–30; 2 Chr. 5:7–10). In both cases, Yahweh responded by filling the Most Holy Place with His glory (Exod. 40:34–35; 2 Chr. 5:11–14). Yet, there is a striking divergence with regard to *when* the glory of Yahweh appeared. In Exodus, the cloud covered the tent as soon as Moses had finished setting up the tabernacle, installing the priests, and offering sacrifice. In 2 Chronicles 5, the glory appears in response to the Levitical song and music:

> And when the priests came forth from the holy place . . . and all the Levitical singers, Asaph, Heman, Jeduthun, and their sons and kinsmen, clothed in fine linen, with cymbals, harps, lyres, standing east of the altar, and with them one hundred and twenty priests blowing trumpets in unison when the trumpeters and the singers were to make themselves heard with one voice to praise and to glorify Yahweh and when they lifted up their voice accompanied by trumpets and cymbals and instruments of music, and when they praised Yahweh, saying, "He indeed is good for His lovingkindness is everlasting," then the house, the house of Yahweh, was filled with a cloud, so that the priests could not stand to minister because of the cloud, for the glory of Yahweh filled the house of God. (2 Chr. 5:11–14; contrast 1 Kgs. 8:10–11)

Chief among the promises memorialized in song was Yahweh's promise to dwell among His people, and at the singing of the Levites He kept His promise. Liturgical music thus does not merely ascend to the heavens as a memorial to a distant God, but calls on God to draw near. And when the praises of the people of God ascend, He descends in glory. Song is not a memorial offered to a distant God; it is performed before the face of His glory. It is a means for calling God to draw near, and an effectual means. Seeking God in song, Israel came upon His glory.

Another passage in the Chronicler's account of the dedication service highlights a different aspect of the connection between music and Yahweh's glory. After Solomon's prayer, fire came from heaven

to consume the ascensions and sacrifices and the Lord's glory filled
the house. In response,

> all the sons of Israel, seeing the fire come down and the glory of Yahweh
> upon the house, bowed down on the pavement with their faces to the
> ground, and they worshiped and gave praise to Yahweh: Truly He is good,
> truly his lovingkindness is everlasting. (2 Chr. 7:3)

In 2 Chronicles 5, music is a means for invoking the Lord's presence, but in chapter 7 praise is a response to the Lord's presence.[21]

One further intriguing consequence seems to follow from this.
In Exodus 29:43, the Lord promised to draw near to Israel, take up
residence within the tent of meeting, and "consecrate the tent with
My glory." The glory of the Lord is the means for consecration;
wherever the Lord is present in glory, that is a holy place, and anyone who serves near the place of the Lord's glory must be "consecrated" to do so. According to the early chapters of Ezekiel, the glory
cloud consists of angelic beings who serve as the Lord's ministers
and carry His traveling throne. When the Lord comes near with His
"holy ones," He consecrates the place.

In Chronicles, however, the courtyard of the temple is called a
"holy place" (2 Chr. 29:7; 35:5),[22] and this means that it is consecrated by the glory of Yahweh. Yet, there is no record that the glory
of Yahweh filled the court. Rather, priests and Levites ministered
there in song and praise and sacrifice. Especially in their capacity as
ministers of music, they formed a created "glory" of Yahweh that
apparently consecrated the court. This is consistent with indications
elsewhere that the hosts of Israel, the hosts of the Lord, formed the
glory that surrounded the throne of Yahweh. Of course, Israel was
not a holy or a consecrating people on her own merits; if the Levites
consecrated the court, it was because they were guided and indwelt
by the Holy Spirit of Yahweh, because their presence in the court was
also the presence of the Spirit. Yet, given that crucial qualification, it

---

[21] For more detailed discussion of both passages, see Kleinig, *The Lord's Song*, 157–170.
[22] Ibid., 94–95.

remains true that the people of God, indwelt by the Spirit of God, consecrate what they touch and make holy the space where they sing.

This is especially evident in Nehemiah. In her 1988 study, *In An Age of Prose: A Literary Approach to Ezra-Nehemiah*,[23] Tamara Eskenazi argues that Ezra and Nehemiah both operate on the assumption that, with the return from exile, the holiness of the temple expanded to include the entire city of Jerusalem. Many bits of evidence support this interpretation. Most directly, Nehemiah called Jerusalem the "holy city" (Neh. 11:1, 18). Eliashib the high priest, moreover, "consecrated" the wall at the beginning of the building project (3:1), and Levites were stationed at the gates of the city (7:1; 13:22), as they had earlier been stationed at the gates of the temple.

The equivalence of the house and the city explains other details of Ezra-Nehemiah as well. The dedication service for the temple is only briefly described (Ezra 6:16–18); compared with the dedication services for Solomon's temple, this feast seems meager indeed. Whatever practical reasons there might have been for limiting the celebration, the theological rationale seems to be that the completion of the temple was not yet the completion of the "house." When we come to the service for the dedication of the city walls, Nehemiah takes several chapters to describe the event. Significantly, the covenant renewal ceremony after the completion of the wall took place in the seventh month (Neh. 8:2), connecting with the completion of the temple of Solomon (1 Kgs. 8:2) since both events were associated with the celebration of the Feast of Booths. After completing the house, moreover, the people committed the sin of Solomon by marrying foreign wives (Neh. 13:26).

The dedication service described in chapter 12 is difficult to follow if one assumes that "house" means "temple." Could all these people fit into the temple court at one time? Further, 12:31–39 describes a double procession around the top of the city wall, with the second stopping at the "Gate of the Guard," but in verse 40 the

[23] Atlanta: Scholars Press.

two choirs are suddenly and inexplicably taking their stand in the "house of God." This is a jarring transition. Either Nehemiah, who has been so careful to describe the procession almost step by step, makes an awkward leap, or something has been dropped from the text, or taking a stand in the "house of God" means standing on the city walls.

One of the striking differences between the "dedication" of the city-house and the earlier dedication of the temple is the absence of the glory cloud. The people bowed to the ground when Ezra blessed the Lord and read the Torah, but no cloud appeared (Neh. 8:6). This was not because the glory-cloud was absent. Rather, the people were the glory-canopy, and their shouts of praise resound through the land (Neh. 12:43). Jerusalem is consecrated as the holy city by the Spirit-filled people of God.[24] Yahweh occupies the holy place through his people's occupation. When Israel occupied the city and filled it with song, the city was consecrated by the glory of Yahweh and became the "holy city."

Overall, the relation between the dedication of the house and the glory develops as follows:

| Sanctuary | Consecration |
|---|---|
| Mosaic tabernacle | Glory-cloud alone |
| Solomon's temple | Glory-cloud *and* chorus |
| Second temple | Chorus alone |
| Church | Chorus alone |

Contrary to the claims of some, Ezra-Nehemiah *does* indicate that the glory returned to the temple after the exile.[25] Instead of a cloud of angels, however, the glory takes the form of a gathering of people; instead of thunder and lightning and a trumpet blast, the glory resounds with cymbals, harps, lyres, and voices.[26]

---

[24] For further discussion, see my article, "The Holy City," *Biblical Horizons* no. 55 (November 1993).

[25] In several places, N. T. Wright has pointed to the absence of the glory as a sign that Israel was still in exile, even though physically in Jerusalem.

[26] This is perhaps supported by Isaiah 30:29–33, which seems to place the "voice of Yahweh" and the song of Israel in poetic parallelism. Israel's song is Yahweh's voice pronouncing judgment against the nations.

Some practical considerations follow from this discussion. First, the musical instruments used at the Davidic tent and Solomon's temple should be noted. They were not merely lyrical, meditative instruments like the harp and lyre, but also cymbals and trumpets. Liturgical orchestras are not required for the church; in many places, congregations will lack talent and funds. But when a church can afford to organize a group of instrumentalists, it should do so. The instrumentation, second, suggests that the music was loud, vigorous, and powerful. The church in song should sound like the glory-cloud that it is—the sound of many waters, a great voice that breaks the cedars of Lebanon, a sound that strikes fear in our enemies.

6. **Song as Edification and Empowerment**. Lest hasty conclusions are drawn from parallels between animal offerings and liturgical song, it is important to notice that other functions of music are also described in Chronicles. Strikingly, the musical ministry of the Levites is described as "prophecy" (1 Chr. 25:1–3), and Heman and Asaph are called seers (1 Chr. 25:5; 2 Chr. 29:30). Various interpretations are offered for this usage, but the most likely is that the singers prophesied by singing God's words. Whatever the precise meaning of this word in this context, prophecy is clearly intended for the edification of the hearer; it is directed toward man, not to God. As Paul pointed out, ecstatic prayer may edify the one praying, but prophecy edifies the church (1 Cor. 14:2–3). Thus, this term applied to liturgical music indicates that the edification of the saints is a valid and necessary consideration in liturgical music. Edification is not the only concern, but even the most beautiful and skillfully performed music is a failure if it ignores the needs of the people of God.

Though edification is not to be equated with good feelings, good feelings should be one of the effects of liturgical music. And "good feelings" here mean "feelings of joy." In his discussion of 2 Chronicles 29:30b ("So they sang praises with joy, and bowed down and worshiped"), Kleinig suggests that the phrase "with joy" means "until there was rejoicing." Thus, "the psalms of David and Asaph are said to have been performed during the presentation of the burnt offering to produce rejoicing."[27] That is, the song was not an expression of joy already achieved, but a means for producing joy. Joy is a fruit of the Spirit, but the Spirit inhabits the praises of the people and is particularly associated with music during the period of the kings (1 Sam. 10:5–6; 2 Kgs. 3:15). Song is one of the Spirit's means for producing His fruits, and the Spirit comes near in glory to fill those who seek Him with gladness. Somber tunes sung at a funereal tempo have their place, and their place is at a funeral. They have little place in the church's worship, that joyful assembly gathered in the heavenly Zion to which we have come.

Along similar lines, the Spirit communicates His *power* through praise (see again 1 Sam. 10). In 2 Chronicles 30:21b, the instruments of music are called "instruments of power." Though this phrase could be understood in a variety of ways,[28] one dimension of its meaning is that the instruments, and the song of the instruments, empowered the singers and musicians.[29] The notion that music empowers is consistent with other features of the Chronicler's theology of song. Song is a memorial, primarily before Yahweh, but also a memorial that reminds the singer of the Lord's mighty acts. As we remember His works in song, our faith is strengthened and we are assured that He will perform similar mighty acts for us. In Deuteronomy, Moses' exhortations to "remember" were not antiquarian; Israel was to remember what Yahweh did to Egypt so they would not fear when they entered to conquer Canaan. In song, the church remembers Egypt, Yahweh's victories over Sihon and Og, His destruction of Jericho and the Philistines, His triumph at Calvary and

---

[27] *The Lord's Song*, 37, with n. 2. Thanks to James Jordan for emphasizing the importance of Kleinig's discussion.

[28] For the various options, see ibid., 88–89.

[29] This is perhaps linked to the Chronicler's description of Levitical ministers in military terms. The gatekeepers are called "mighty men" or "men of valor" (1 Chr. 26:6–9), and the priests and Levites are, like the members of the military, distributed in "divisions" (1 Chr. 24:1; 23:6). For further discussion of these passages, see ibid., 170. Though I have found no passages that refer to musicians as "mighty men," the idea may be at work in the passages that describe Israel's warfare through song (esp. 2 Chr. 20:1–3; see ibid., 170–180 for a detailed discussion of this passage).

in the resurrection—and as we remember in song we know more and more confidently that the same God will do the same for us. Further, the psalm of praise that accompanied the ascension of the ark exhorts Israel to "seek Yahweh and His strength" (1 Chr. 16:11). Since song was a means for "seeking Yahweh," it is also a means for seeking His power.[30] And those who seek—who seek according to the ordinance—will find.

The psychological fact is undeniable. Song can turn melancholy into joy, and weakness to overwhelming power. But this insight has played little role in Reformed discussions of liturgical music. Chronicles indicates that this is not merely a "psychological fact," but part of God's revelation about music. We sing "until there is rejoicing" with "instruments that produce power." Through song the Spirit builds up the body of Christ and produces His fruit.

7. **Qualifications for Musical Ministers**. Given the fact that song is a means of edification, it is natural to expect that song leaders should be qualified for their task. This point is brought home by the Chronicler's description of Hezekiah's Passover,

> And the sons of Israel present in Jerusalem celebrated the Feast of Unleavened bread seven days with great joy, and the Levites and priests praised Yahweh day after day with instruments of power of Yahweh. Then Hezekiah spoke to the heart of all the Levites who showed good understanding of Yahweh. So they ate for the appointed seven days, sacrificing peace offerings and giving thanks to Yahweh God of their fathers. (2 Chr. 30:21–22)

The important phrase here is the description of the Levites as men "who showed good understanding of Yahweh." Both the verb and the noun in this clause are from the same word group, so that a more literal rendition would be "Levites who understood good understanding of Yahweh." Kleinig suggests that the clause is deliberately ambiguous:

> On the one hand, the skill of the musicians in their performance of the sacred song showed the depth of their insight into the Lord. On the other

---

[30] Ibid., 88.

hand, by the skillful rendition of their anthems, they communicated their insight to the people and so taught them, affectively as well as cognitively, about the Lord and his goodness through their musical performance of praise.[31]

Two sets of implications follow from this passage. First, song is a means for passing on wisdom. By singing, we grow in our "good understanding of Yahweh." Several passages from the Psalms reinforce this idea. Psalm 49 begins with an exhortation to the nations to hear the psalmist because "My mouth will speak wisdom; and the meditation of my heart will be understanding. I will incline my ear to a proverb; I will open up my riddle on the harp" (vv. 3–4). The latter phrase does not simply mean that the song will "propose" or "express" the riddle (as in the NASB translation). Rather, the harp is a means for "resolving" the riddle; the verb means to "open up" or even "unlock," and the instrument is the key by which this particular riddle will be opened. Similarly, Asaph calls on Israel to "listen . . . to my *torah*," since in his song he promised to open his mouth in parables, and utter "dark sayings of old" (Ps. 78:1–2).[32] Importantly, these passages do not simply say that singing is a means for transferring theological information; rather, singing inculcates wisdom and unlocks the mysteries of God's works.

Second, this passage indicates that those who select and lead music must be men with "good understanding of Yahweh." If music is intended to give pleasure to Yahweh, then it is essential that those who lead music understand what gives Yahweh pleasure. They must know His musical "tastes." And, of course, since song is a communicator of wisdom, those who determine the musical direction of the church must grasp the difference between wisdom and folly. Musical ministry should not be handed over to whichever church

---

[31] Ibid., 76.

[32] These passages are cited and discussed by J. H. Eaton, "Music's Place in Worship: A Contribution from the Psalms," in *Prophetism, Worship and Theodicy: Studies in Prophetism, Biblical Theology and Rhetorical Analysis and on the Place of Music in Worship* (Leiden: Brill, 1984), 101–102. Eaton suggests that the verbs translated "muse" and "meditate" in the Psalms have musical connotation; he translates Psalm 1:2 as "from his law he intones day and night," and Psalm 119:97 as "How I love your law! It is my chant all the day."

member who can plunk out a few chords on the piano. It should instead be seen as a ministerial office, reserved for those with theological training, spiritual maturity, and "good understanding of Yahweh." Reformed churches have historically lagged far behind Lutheran and Anglican churches in their musical skill, and ordaining theologically and musically trained men to music ministry would be one way of correcting this weakness.[33]

A similar conclusion follows from the notion that Levitical musicians were given "guard duty." This suggests that their music had some kind of conserving purpose, not only reminding God of His covenant, but ensuring that the covenant was remembered and kept (guarded) from generation to generation in Israel. Levites were not simply assigned to "guard the instruments," but apparently their musical ministry, their songs and performances, were themselves a means for guarding the people. A song is an effective means for preserving stories and wisdom, and for passing it to one's children. I cannot remember much about elementary or junior high school, but I can still sing "Joshua fit the battle of Jericho" and "Rock-a-my soul in the bosom of Abraham" and other folk songs, not to mention dozens of pop tunes that I'd prefer to forget.

If liturgical music is to perform this role, it seems that its musical style should change slowly, not attempting to keep pace with every fad of entertainment music. Much contemporary Christian music seems to me to fail in this conserving function; it does not pass on the faith and piety of previous generations, and it does not maintain the musical tone of previous generations. Musicians are not only failing to guard the tradition of church music, but through this failure are failing to use their musical ministry to guard the church.

---

[33] Of course, many churches will not be able to support a full time or even a part time music minister. But it should be the goal of even small churches to have a theologically trained music leader as soon as they are able. Leadership in music ministry should take high priority: Before the youth director or the counseling pastor, before the expansion of the parking lot, before the purchase of an organ, a church should be seeking out a theologically trained musician.

8. **Song as Mission.** The Chronicler also frequently describes
music as a form of "making known"—as proclamation and preaching. The verb used with "cymbals" is a form of the verb *shema'*, one
that means "to cause to hear" or "to sound out" (1 Chr. 15:19; 16:5).
Through their song, the Levites at David's tent were to "make
known His deeds among the people" (16:8). Kleinig points out the
parallel between 16:8 and Exodus 33:19, where Yahweh "proclaims"
His name to Moses. In their song, the Levites join the chorus of the
glory-cloud, another indication that the chorus is a human form of
the glory.[34] He also points out the variety of synonyms for song
found in the psalm in 1 Chronicles 16, i.e., *proclaim, publicize, muse
on, announce, relate, say* (vv. 8–9, 23–24, 31).[35] Israel's song was
"about Yahweh," and indeed, He was so much the content of their
psalms that the psalmist could say "My song is Yah" (118:14).

Specifically, Israel is to proclaim the "name" of Yahweh. Israel is
exhorted to "call upon His name" (1 Chr. 16:8), to "glory" in it
(16:10), and to "give thanks" to it (16:35). By doing this, they were
also calling the nations to join in to "ascribe to Yahweh the glory
due His name" (16:29). As elsewhere in the Old Testament, the
"name" of Yahweh includes not only the bare syllables, but His attributes, works, mercies, promises and performance of promises. All
of that is proclaimed when Yahweh's name is proclaimed.[36] Commonly in the ancient world, song celebrated the deeds of great he-
roes, and there is an analogy with that idea in Israel's celebration of
Yahweh's works. Just as the women sang praises to Saul and David
as they returned from battle, so the bride, Israel, celebrated Yahweh's
prowess—for if Saul has killed his thousands and David his ten
thousands, Yahweh has killed myriads of myriads.[37]

---

[34] Kleinig, *The Lord's Song*, 65, n. 1.
[35] Ibid., 145.
[36] This previous paragraph is based on Kleinig's discussion in ibid., 145.
[37] See the interesting iconographic reflection of this in Othmar Keel, *The Symbolism of the
Biblical World: Ancient Near Eastern Iconography and the Book of Psalms* (trans. Timothy J.
Hallett; New York: Crossroad, 1985), 338, fig. 451. The picture shows Horus defeating
Seth, crossing the river in a boat, and being greeted on the far side by women with tambou-
rines.

9. **The Liturgical Placement of Song**: Another set of conclusions has to do with the actual liturgical placement of music. 2 Chronicles 29:20–35, which describes Hezekiah's rededication of the temple, is particularly important here. Sacrifices were offered in the normal sequence: first a purification of seven bulls, seven rams, seven lamps and seven male goats (v. 21); then an ascension consisting of 70 bulls, 100 rams, 200 lambs (vv. 25–28, 32), and finally communion sacrifices (v. 31). It is important to note how music fit into this sequence. No music was played during the purification offering, but after it was completed, Hezekiah set up the Levites and priests:

> And the Levites stood with the instruments of David, and the priests with the trumpets. Then Hezekiah gave the order to offer the ascension on the altar. When the ascension began, the song to Yahweh also began with the trumpets, and according to the authority of the instruments of David, king of Israel. While the whole assembly worshiped, the singers also sang and the trumpets sounded; all this until the ascension was complete. Now at the completion of the ascensions, the king and all the people who were present with him bowed down and worshiped. Moreover, king Hezekiah and the officials ordered the Levites to sing praises to Yahweh with the words of David and Asaph the seer. So they sang praises with joy, and bowed down and worshiped. (vv. 26–30)

The coordination of the singing with the ascension offering makes theological sense. Song, normally an expression of joy, would not be appropriate during the offering of a purification offering.[38] Ascensions, however, represented the worshiper's self-consecration to Yahweh, and also his ascension into the presence of God, and the parallel of music with the ascension indicates that music too is a means of ascension. In Christian worship, the ascension in song

---

[38] My colleague Duck Schuler objects that this leaves no place for penitential psalms. Such psalms, which are common in Scripture, might be used in several ways. First, many penitential psalms begin in mourning and move toward joy (e.g., Ps. 22; and even 51), and these would fit well after the absolution, as the church moves from its confession of sin into an ascension of praise. Second, other psalms might be used at particular times of the church year, for the tone of worship need not be uniform (though it should, in the main, be joyous). Third, these psalms might be *said* as confessions. Finally, I do not believe that a church is in grievous sin if the confession is sung, but it should not be the norm.

would best take place after the absolution; having been declared for-
given, the people of God burst out in praise, thanks, and memorializing the name of Yahweh and of Jesus.[39] Once the absolution is
sounded, the people begin to ascend in song into the heavenly places.

In the Psalms, furthermore, song is sometimes associated with
the peace offering, also known as sacrifices or thank offerings:

> And now my head will be lifted up above my enemies around me; and I
> will offer in His tent sacrifices of shouts of joy; I will sing, yes, I will sing
> praises to Yahweh. (Ps. 27:6)

> Let them give thanks to Yahweh for His lovingkindness, and for His won-
> ders to the sons of men. Let them also offer sacrifices of thanksgiving, and
> tell of His works with joyful singing. (Ps. 107:21–22)

Not only is song understood under the description of an ascension offering, but it is also seen as analogous to the "sacrifice" or
"peace offering."

In New Covenant worship, the peace offering is fulfilled in the
Lord's Supper, and these passages indicate that song during the
celebration of the Lord's Supper is appropriate and good. Much eucharistic music, however, is far too slow, meditative, and melancholy,
contributing powerfully to a eucharistic piety that treats the Supper
as "tomb" rather than "table." Meditative music might occasionally
be used at the Supper, but I believe that vigorous and triumphal music
is far more appropriate. The Supper is a victory meal, memorializing
the death that vanquished the powers and led captivity captive. It is
not a moment to wallow in sorrow, but a moment to celebrate
Christ the Victor. The picture we should have of eucharistic celebration is not an assembly of people bowed with eyes closed; we should
think of a mead hall, with loud song, shouts, joyful noise. Surely,
this was the atmosphere of Old Testament festivals, for Yahweh
commonly exhorted Israel to rejoice greatly in their feasts.[40]

---

[39] I agree with Kleinig's point that song is not a means of atonement, but a response of
thanks and praise to the announcement of atonement achieved.

[40] Schuler again objects: since the Supper is a memorial and proclamation of Christ's death,
more somber songs have their place. As with singing confessions, I do not believe that it is

*So What? Song and Redemptive History*

Whenever Israel moved closer to her "end," her "eschaton," Davidic music revived. Hezekiah revived the music ministry of the temple, instituted by David with instruments, singers, trumpets (2 Chr. 29:25–28). When Josiah restored the temple of the Lord, he also reorganized the priests according to the order instituted by David (2 Chr. 35:4), and when he restored the temple, the singers joined the celebration (35:15). The rebuilt temple was a place of singing and praise, as was the foundation of the temple, and finishing of the whole city (Ezra 2:65; 3:10–11; Neh. 12:24, 27, 36, 44–47). In each case, the restoration of Israel was accompanied by a restoration of music in worship. At the center of the Chronicler's world stands the Levitical choir, and they stand at the end as well. History moves toward song, through the instrumentality of song.

In the course of this book, I have noted several times that the establishment of song marked the ascension of the ark into David's tent as an eschatological event. And so it always is—song comes at the end, when the Lord has come near to save His people. Israel sings about Pharaoh sinking like a stone after they are safely across the sea, the heavens burst into praise when the Lamb comes forward to receive all power and glory and majesty and dominion, and the saints proclaim Hallelujahs when it is confirmed that the whore is slain.

If these things have not happened, the end has not yet come and we have nothing to sing about. Let's hang our harps on the willows along the streams of Babylon and be silent forever.

But the church is singing, and always has been singing, and that can only mean that we are witnesses not only to the beginning of the end but to the end of the beginning. Because we are witnesses of the end, the end that has already begun in Jesus, we are so confident of the final outcome that we have begun the celebration a bit prematurely—by, say, several dozen millennia. Song is an act of faith, eschatological faith that David's tent has been raised, that Zion is exalted as chief of the mountains, that the nations are streaming

---

grave sin for a church to sing "O Sacred Head" during communion. But I do not believe that the mourning should be the dominant note struck.

to worship there. And it is only men and women of faith who will see these promises realized more and more fully—that is to say, only men and women of song.

# Scripture Index

## Genesis

3:15  74
4:7  59
9:14–15  114
14:14  47
14:20  96
17:23  47
22  17
23  25
32:4–5, 7  47
46:26–27  47
49:3  59

## Exodus

1:1–5  47
3:15  103
6:14–27  48
12:38  47
15:1–18  50
15:1–21  116
19:16, 19  55
25–31  26
25–40  33
25:17–22  82
25:9, 40  26
26:30  26

29:10–34  108
29:41–42  70
29:43  118
33:7–11  27
33:19  126
35–40  26
40:5  35
40:12–16  117
40:20–30  117
40:29  117
40:34–35  117

## Leviticus

1:5–6  99
1:8  99
1:9  99
2:2, 9, 16  114
5:12  114
5:14–6:7  54
7:15–18  108
8:14–29  108
9:24  25
16:2, 14  35
16:21  14, 54
21:16–24  102
23  54
23:2–3  54

23:37  71

## Numbers

1:53  65
3–9  26
3:7  65
3:39  47
4:1–20  67
4:15  59
4:19  60
4:19–20  39
4:21–28  67
4:24  60, 62
4:27  60, 62
4:29–33  67
4:31  62
4:32  60
4:47  60
4:49  60, 62
6:16–17  108
8:26  65
10:9–10  14, 68, 69, 103
10:10  54
13:6  47
15:11–16  38
16:9  64
18:3–5  65
28:1–8  108
28:3–4  70
28:6  70
28:10  70
28:15, 24, 31  70
29:1–38  108
29:6, 11, 16  70
32:12  47

## Deuteronomy

10:8  57, 58, 59, 64
12  31, 55
14:23–24  31

16:6, 11, 15  31
17:12  64
18:5  57, 64
18:5, 7  102
28:64–68  74
31:6–7, 23  27

## Joshua

1:7, 9, 18  27
2:8–13  50
9:17  39
9:27  39
13:3  41
14:6  47
14:14  47
15:9, 60  39
18:1  19
19:45  41
21:16  39
21:24–25  41

## Judges

5:1–31  50
5:5  116
5:19–31  116

## 1 Samuel

2:10  51
2:29, 32  83
4–6  13, 43, 91
4:1–7:2  12
4:4  82
6:10–12  39
6:10–21  39
6:19–7:2  92
7:1–2  39
7:14  42
10:5–6  122
16–31  20

16:8  39
17:4  41
27:1–7  42
29:6–10  42
31:2  39
31:7  42

## 2 Samuel

2–4  21
2–5, 8  23
5–8  19
5:1–5  21
5:6–10  21, 22
5:7  11
5:9, 11  83
5:11–16  22
5:17–25  22
6  13, 19, 42
6:1  13
6:1–5  92
6:1–11  22
6:2  82
6:3  40
6:6–11  92
6:10  41
6:12–19  22, 92
6:17  31, 33, 79
6:20–23  22
7:1  79
7:1–29  22
7:2  79
7:11  77
7:18  36, 95
8:1–14  92
8:11  24
11:1  23, 78
11:11  77, 78, 79
12:26  23
15:18  42
15:18–19  41

15:21  42
18:2  41
21:2  40
21:19  41
23  23
23:8–39  21
24  24, 25
24:5–7  78

## 1 Kings

3:14  27
3:15  55
6:38–7:1  112
8:1  11
8:1–11  13
8:2  119
8:10–11  117
8:11  64
9:4  27
20:12  77

## 2 Kings

3:15  122
14:25  41
25  17

## 1 Chronicles

1:1–2:2  28
1:1–27  28
2:3–4:23  28
2:50, 52  39
4:23–43  28
5  28
6  28
6:1–16  29
6:17–30  29
6:29  40
6:31  29, 83
6:31–32  61

6:31–33a 64
6:31–47 29
6:33–47 68
6:39 45
6:48 29
6:49 26
6:49–53 29
6:69 41
7 28
8 28
8:7 40
9:1–34 28
9:17–27 44
9:28–29 66
10 21
10:1–14 20
10:13–14 113
10:14 21
11–12 21
11:1 21
11:3 21
11:4–7 22
11:4–9 21
11:5 11
11:10–47 21
11:41 23
12:1 21
12:1–22 21
12:23–37 21
12:38 21
13–16 13, 19, 22
13:1–14 22
13:8 36
13:10 36
13:13 41, 46
13:13–14 44
13:14 46
14:1–7 22
14:8–17 22, 38
15–16 24, 43
15:1 31, 33

15:1–15 22, 58
15:1–16:3 58
15:1–16:43 22, 58
15:1–24 22
15:2 40, 57, 58, 59
15:3 22, 58
15:3–16:3 58
15:4–15 58
15:13 40, 113
15:15 26, 58
15:16 64, 66
15:16, 28 66
15:16–16:3 58
15:16–24 59
15:16–25 58
15:17 64
15:18 44
15:18, 24 43
15:19 126
15:22 60
15:24 66
15:24–25 44
15:25 44
15:25–16:3 58
15:25–28 55
15:27 60, 61
16 51, 99
16:1 13, 36, 55
16:4 35, 43, 65, 68, 115
16:4, 37 59
16:4–6 22, 55, 59
16:4–43 58, 59
16:5 66, 126
16:6 35
16:6, 42 66
16:7–36 59
16:8 126
16:8–9 115, 126
16:8–36 48, 115
16:9 48
16:10 126

16:11  113, 123
16:12, 15  115
16:16–17  115
16:19–20  115
16:21  115
16:23–24  126
16:24  115
16:29  126
16:30  115
16:31  126
16:34–36  115
16:35  126
16:36b  66
16:37  35, 45, 55, 68, 70
16:37–38  22
16:37–43  22, 56, 59, 80
16:38  43, 45
16:39–40  33, 54
16:39–42  94
16:39–43  13
16:40  70
16:41–42  54, 68
16:43  22, 58
17:1–27  22
17:16  36
9:16  45
20:1  23
20:5  41
21  24
21:26  25
22:1  25
22:13  27
22:14–16  24
23–27  24
23–29  24
23:1–2  24
23:2–26:32  24
23:6  122
23:25–32  62
23:26  66
23:30–32  71

23:32  78
24:1  122
25:1, 3, 6  66
25:1–3  121
25:1–31  55
25:2  112
25:5  121
25:6  36
25:8  65
26:1–2, 9  45
26:1–5  45
26:4–5, 8, 15  43
26:6–9  122
27:1–34  24
28:1–29:30  24
28:10, 20  27
28:13  57
28:13–14  66
28:14, 17  66
28:19  24, 26, 56
29:1–5  24
35:3  63
35:15  63

## 2 Chronicles

3:1  11, 14, 17, 24, 25, 32
4:1–22  33
4:16  66
5:1  25
5:2  11
5:2–10  32
5:2–14  13
5:5  33, 66
5:6  117
5:7–10  117
5:11  117
5:11–14  55, 117
5:14  64
6:4–6  25
7:3  118

7:6  55, 112
8:12–13  26, 71
8:13–14  26
8:14  26, 114
11:16  113
17:3–4  114
19:3  114
20:1–3  122
20:3–4  114
20:11  112
23:13  55
23:18  26
24:6, 9  26
25:24  43
26:11  112
29:7  118
29:11  64
29:20–35  127
29:20–36  108
29:25  57
29:25–28  55, 129
29:25–30  63
29:30  121
29:30b  121
29:35  63
30:21–22  123
30:21b  122
31:13  112
34:12  55
35:4  26, 129
35:5  118
35:6  26
35:15  26, 129

## Ezra

2:65  129
3:1–6  27
3:4  71
3:10–11  129
4:24  27

6:13–18  27
6:16–18  119

## Nehemiah

3:1  119
7:1  119
8:2  119
8:6  120
11:1, 18  119
12:24  129
12:27  129
12:31–39  119
12:36  129
12:43  120
12:44–47  129
13:22  119
13:26  119

## Job

13:11  59
31:32  59

## Psalms

1:2  124
17:8  81
18:49  51
22  127
22:3  61
22:22  112
22:27  51
27  82
27:4  14, 80
27:4–6  79
27:6  128
31  82
31:19–21  81
47:1  51
49:3–4  124
51  127

57:9 51
61:4 82
62:5 59
67:3–5 51
76:1–3 82
78:1–2 124
107:21–22 128
110:4 96
117:1 51
118:14 126
119:97 124
132:13–14 31

## Isaiah

1:8 83
16:5 37, 95
30:29–33 120
56:6–7 51
66:18–21 51
66:22 52

## Jeremiah

12:7–15 90
52 17, 91

## Ezekiel

44:11, 15 64

## Amos

1–6 84
1:1 83
1:2 84
2:16 87
3:1 84
4:1 84
5:1 84
5:1–17 83, 84
5:1–2 85
5:1–6:14 83, 84, 85, 87, 88

5:1–7 85
5:7 84
5:8–15 85
5:8–9 85
5:11 86
5:16–6:8 85
5:18 84, 86
5:18–19 86
5:18–6:14 84
5:19 87
5:21–22 88
5:23 88
5:26 87
5:27 87
6:1 88
6:1–3 87
6:5 88
6:5–6 88
6:8 87, 88
6:8–14 85
6:12 84
6:14 87
7:1 84
7:1, 4, 7 85
7:4 84
7:7 84
8:1 84, 85
8:4 84
9:1 74, 84, 85, 87
9:1–15 85, 87, 88
9:1–4 92
9:1–5 83
9:3 86
9:3–4 74
9:4 87
9:5 87
9:5–6 86
9:7 75, 87
9:7–10 92
9:9 75
9:9–15 76

9:11   76, 77, 78, 83, 85, 87, 88, 91
9:11–12   16, 73, 76, 78, 83, 87, 91, 95
9:11–15   86, 92
9:12   77
9:13   86
9:13–15   75
9:14   75, 86
9:15   75

## Malachi

3:7   91

## Matthew

26:30   112

## Luke

24:50–53   100

## Acts

10–11   90
10:1ff   98
10:47   90
11:20   89
14:26–28   89
15:1–2   89
15:8–9   90
15:12–21   73
15:13–18   76
15:16   77
15:16–18   16, 78, 90
15:17   91
15:29   90
21:26   100

## Romans

11:11, 14   93
11:12   93

## 1 Corinthians

14:2–3   121

## Ephesians

2:6   99

## Hebrews

2:12   113
4:11–12   108
7   47
7:4–9   96
7:11   97
7:11–28   96
9:2–5   34
9:8–10   34
13:15   106

## 1 John

1:8–9   108

## Revelation

5:1–14   112
20:4   99